THE MISSIO DEI BREVIARY

www.thebreviary.com

a four week breviary with morning and evening prayers

by Missio Dei
Minneapolis, Minnesota
www.missio-dei.com

Published in the United States of America by
MISSIO DEI
Minneapolis, MN 55454

Edited and designed by Mark Van Steenwyk

ISBN 978-0-6151-8804-1

For an online version of this breviary, visit www.thebreviary.com.

Free or discounted copies available upon request.

Contents

Introduction

This breviary is the work of a small community in Minneapolis called "Missio Dei." Missio Dei is a religious order of sorts—a community of hospitality, peace, and prayer that exists to embody Jesus Christ on the West Bank of Minneapolis. The West Bank is a neighborhood of immigrants and punks and artists and homeless people and students and professionals. Though it is a small neighborhood of roughly a square mile, more than 8000 people live there with many others studying, working, or recreating there.

We are an Anabaptist community that is inspired by the Franciscan Tradition, a part of the New Monastic Movement, and fluent in the emerging church conversation. In short, we are the fruit of diverse traditions.

The problem with being influenced by many traditions is that one can easily develop a consumer mindset. It is too common, these days, to simply "shop" around for convictions. We treat religion like a shopping mall, picking and choosing what things we want to adopt as religious practices. And in the Great Mall of Religion, even Jesus can become merely a product.

We are convinced that the only way to resist the consumer mindset is to submit to something outside one's self. As a community, we try to submit to one another. And as a community, we try to submit to Scripture, the Holy Spirit, and shared spiritual rhythms. This book of prayer lays the foundation for these shared spiritual rhythms.

The Missio Dei Breviary reflects our deepest-held convictions. The central emphasis is Christ. The reflections demonstrate a missional commitment to place and a focused commitment to social justice—within an Anabaptist theological perspective.

What follows are morning and evening for 28 days. The first week focuses on chapter 5 of Matthew. Week two focuses on Luke's parables. Week three emphasizes the seven signs and seven "I am" statements found in John. Week 4 follows Mark's account of the final week of Jesus—from his entry into Jerusalem through his trial, crucifixion, and resurrection.

The morning prayers include a set of opening prayers (borrowing from the Eastern Orthodox tradition), a Scripture reading, the Lord's Prayer, and a closing prayer. The evening prayers are similar, but contain a call to praise (drawing from the Great Commandment) instead of an opening prayer and replace the Lord's Prayer with one of seven different scriptural canticles. The evening prayer also includes a psalm.

Some of the canticles used within the breviary are traditional: the Magnificat, Zechariah's Prophecy, Simeon's Song, and the Gloria. Two canticles have been included that, while not usually included in traditional books of prayer, are Scriptural songs: the kenosis hymn from Philippians 2 (which we call "Paul's Song") and a song from Revelation 5 (which we call "the Song Around the Throne"). Besides these six canticles, we include a prayer called "the Jesus Manifesto" which draws upon Luke 4:18-19.

We recommend that you pray the morning prayer when you first arise. Evening prayer is best prayed before or after dinner, when you are likely to be with friends or family. While this book can be used as a personal devotional book, it is intended to be used by 2 or more people together.

For each reading, we suggest that you pause for a while between sections in each. During the reflection (which is italicized), allow several minutes for prayer or silent reflection. Please take your time.

Our hope and prayer is that this little book will be a blessing to you. It has already been a blessing to us.

week one:

the
sermon
on the
mount

Week 1: Sunday Morning

In the morning, before you begin the day, stand with reverence before the All-Seeing God and say:

(+) In the Name of the Father, and of the Son, and of the Holy Spirit. Amen.

Having invoked the Holy Trinity, keep silence for a little while, so that your thoughts and feelings may be freed from worldly cares. Then recite the following prayers without haste, and with your whole heart.

The Tax Collector's Prayer

God, have mercy on me, a sinner.

Opening Prayer

Lord, open our lips and our mouths will proclaim your praise.
You are good to those who wait for you, to all who seek you.

Matthew 5:3

Blessed are the poor in spirit,
for the kingdom of heaven belongs to them.

James 2:5

Listen, my dear brothers and sisters! Did not God choose the poor in the world to be rich in faith and heirs of the kingdom that he promised to those who love him?

Jeremiah 22:16

"He upheld the cause of the poor and needy. So things went well for Judah." The Lord says, "That is a good example of what it means to know me."

Pray for the poor.

The Lord's Prayer

Our Father in heaven,
hallowed be your name,

may your kingdom come,
may your will be done
on earth as it is in heaven.

Give us today our daily bread.

And forgive us our debts,
as we ourselves have forgiven our debtors.

And do not lead us into temptation,
but deliver us from the evil one.
For yours is the kingdom and the power and the glory forever.

Amen.

Closing Prayer

Heavenly Father, grant us humility of spirit. Give us the faith to love the poor, the widow, the orphan, and the oppressed as you do, and to be of the same spirit as "the least of these." Lord, replace all pride in our lives with true humility. Teach us to walk today, humbly trusting in you as we share your love in word and deed.

We ask this through our Lord Jesus Christ, your Son, who lives and reigns with you and the Holy Spirit, one God, for ever and ever. Amen.

Week 1: Sunday Evening

Call to Praise

After a time of reflective silence, proclaim:

"Love the Lord your God with all your heart and with all your soul and with all your mind." This is the first and greatest commandment. And the second is like it: "Love your neighbor as yourself." All the Law and the Prophets hang on these two commandments.

Psalm 42

For the music director; a well-written song by the Korahites.

As the deer longs for streams of water,
so I long for you, O God!

I thirst for God, for the living God.
I say, "When will I be able to go and appear in God's presence?"

I cannot eat,
I weep day and night;
all day long they say to me,
"Where is your God?"

I will remember and weep!
For I was once walking along with the great throng
to the temple of God,
shouting and giving thanks
along with the crowd as we celebrated the holy festival.

Why are you depressed, O my soul?
Why are you upset?
Wait for God!
For I will again give thanks
to my God for his saving intervention.

I am depressed,
so I will pray to you while I am trapped
here in the region of the upper Jordan,
from Hermon, from Mount Mizar.

One deep stream calls out to another
at the sound of your waterfalls;
all your billows and waves overwhelm me.

By day the Lord decrees his loyal love,
and by night he gives me a song,
a prayer to the living God.

I will pray to God, my high ridge:
"Why do you ignore me?
Why must I walk around mourning
because my enemies oppress me?"

My enemies' taunts cut into me to the bone,
as they say to me all day long, "Where is your God?"

Why are you depressed, O my soul?
Why are you upset?
Wait for God!
For I will again give thanks
to my God for his saving intervention.

Matthew 5:4

Blessed are those who mourn,
for they will be comforted.

Revelations 21:3-5a

And I heard a loud voice from the throne saying, "Look! The residence of God is among human beings. He will live among them, and they will be his people, and God himself will be with them. He will wipe away every tear from their eyes, and death will not exist any more—or mourning, or crying, or pain, for the former things have ceased to exist.

And the one seated on the throne said: "Look! I am making all things new!"

Ask God to comfort those who mourn; pray especially for those in your neighborhood who mourn.

The Jesus Manifesto

With Jesus, we proclaim:

> *The Spirit of the Lord is upon me,*
> *because he has anointed me*
> *to proclaim good news to the poor.*
> *He has sent me to proclaim release to the captives*
> *and the regaining of sight to the blind,*
> *to set free those who are oppressed,*
> *to proclaim the year of the Lord's favor.*

Father, anoint us with your Spirit. As you sent your Son, your Son has sent us; may we embody the presence of your Son in the world, and in our neighborhood. Empower us to live and proclaim your good news in our neighborhood, and in the world.

Closing Prayer

Lord, bring comfort to those who mourn in our neighborhood. Help us to show them love, help us to comfort them.

We ask this through our Lord Jesus Christ, your Son, who lives and reigns with you and the Holy Spirit, one God, for ever and ever. Amen.

Week 1: Monday Morning

In the morning, before you begin the day, stand with reverence before the All-Seeing God and say:

(+) In the Name of the Father, and of the Son, and of the Holy Spirit. Amen.

Having invoked the Holy Trinity, keep silence for a little while, so that your thoughts and feelings may be freed from worldly cares. Then recite the following prayers without haste, and with your whole heart.

The Tax Collector's Prayer

God, have mercy on me, a sinner.

Opening Prayer

Lord, open our lips and our mouths will proclaim your praise.
You are good to those who wait for you, to all who seek you.

Matthew 5:5

Blessed are the meek, for they will inherit the earth.

Colossians 3:12-15

Therefore, as the elect of God, holy and dearly loved, clothe yourselves with a heart of mercy, kindness, humility, gentleness, and patience, bearing with one another and forgiving one another, if someone happens to have a complaint against anyone else. Just as the Lord has forgiven you, so you also forgive others. And to all these virtues add love, which is the perfect bond. Let the peace of Christ be in control in your heart (for you were in fact called as one body to this peace), and be thankful.

Take this time to forgive those who have wronged you, and reflect upon those whom you have wronged.

The Lord's Prayer

Our Father in heaven,
hallowed be your name,

may your kingdom come,
may your will be done
on earth as it is in heaven.

Give us today our daily bread.

And forgive us our debts,
as we ourselves have forgiven our debtors.

And do not lead us into temptation,
but deliver us from the evil one.
For yours is the kingdom and the power and the glory forever.

Amen.

Closing Prayer

Lord, may we be built up in our most holy faith by your Holy
Spirit. Keep us in your love as we wait for the mercy of our Lord
Jesus Christ to bring us eternal life.

We ask this through our Lord Jesus Christ, your Son, who lives
and reigns with you and the Holy Spirit, one God, for ever and
ever. Amen.

Week 1: Monday Evening

Call to Praise

After a time of reflective silence, proclaim:

"Love the Lord your God with all your heart and with all your
soul and with all your mind." This is the first and greatest
commandment. And the second is like it: "Love your neighbor as
yourself." All the Law and the Prophets hang on these two
commandments.

Psalm 140

For the music director; a psalm of David.

O Lord, rescue me from wicked men!
Protect me from violent men,
who plan ways to harm me.

All day long they stir up conflict.
Their tongues wound like a serpent;
a viper's venom is behind their lips. (Selah)

O Lord, shelter me from the power of the wicked!
Protect me from violent men,
who plan to knock me over.

Proud men hide a snare for me;
evil men spread a net by the path;
they set traps for me. (Selah)

I say to the Lord, "You are my God."
O Lord, pay attention to my plea for mercy!
O sovereign Lord, my strong deliverer,
you shield my head in the day of battle.

O Lord, do not let the wicked have their way!
Do not allow their plan to succeed when they attack! (Selah)

As for the heads of those who surround me—
may the harm done by their lips overwhelm them!
May he rain down fiery coals upon them!
May he throw them into the fire!
From bottomless pits they will not escape.

A slanderer will not endure on the earth;
calamity will hunt down a violent man and strike him down.

I know that the Lord defends the cause of the oppressed
and vindicates the poor.

Certainly the godly will give thanks to your name;
the morally upright will live in your presence.

Matthew 5:6

Blessed are those who hunger and thirst for righteousness, for
they will be satisfied.

*Reflect upon the injustices of this world. Reflect upon the un-
righteousness in your heart. Confess them to the Lord and ask
for his justice to prevail.*

Mary's Song

My soul exalts the Lord,
and my spirit has begun to rejoice in God my Savior,

because he has looked upon
the humble state of his servant.
For from now on all generations will call me blessed,

because He-Who-is-Mighty has done great things for me,
holy is his name.

He is merciful to those who fear him,
from generation to generation.

He has demonstrated power with his arm;
he has scattered those whose pride wells up from the sheer
arrogance of their hearts.

He has brought down the mighty from their thrones,
and has lifted up those of lowly position;

he has filled the hungry with good things,
and has sent the rich away empty.

He has helped his servant Israel,
remembering his mercy,

as he promised to our ancestors,
to Abraham and to his descendants forever.

Closing Prayer

Lord, may we never be satisfied with the justice and
righteousness of this world. Stir us from our apathy as we cry for
your justice.

We ask this through our Lord Jesus Christ, your Son, who lives
and reigns with you and the Holy Spirit, one God, for ever and
ever. Amen.

Week 1: Tuesday Morning

In the morning, before you begin the day, stand with reverence before the All-Seeing God and say:

(+) In the Name of the Father, and of the Son, and of the Holy Spirit. Amen.

Having invoked the Holy Trinity, keep silence for a little while, so that your thoughts and feelings may be freed from worldly cares. Then recite the following prayers without haste, and with your whole heart.

The Tax Collector's Prayer

God, have mercy on me, a sinner.

Opening Prayer

Lord, open our lips and our mouths will proclaim your praise.
You are good to those who wait for you, to all who seek you.

Matthew 5:7

Blessed are the merciful, for they will be shown mercy.

Ephesians 2:4-10

But God, being rich in mercy, because of his great love with which he loved us, even though we were dead in transgressions, made us alive together with Christ—by grace you are saved. And he raised us up with him and seated us with him in the heavenly realms in Christ Jesus, to demonstrate in the coming ages the surpassing wealth of his grace in kindness toward us in Christ Jesus. For by grace you are saved through faith, and this is not from yourselves, it is the gift of God; it is not from works, so that no one can boast. For we are his workmanship, having been created in Christ Jesus for good works that God prepared beforehand so that we might walk in them.

Confess your sins to the Lord, calling upon him for his mercy. Confess your sins to one another, and if any have sinned against you, extend mercy to them.

The Lord's Prayer

Our Father in heaven,
hallowed be your name,

may your kingdom come,
may your will be done
on earth as it is in heaven.

Give us today our daily bread.

And forgive us our debts,
as we ourselves have forgiven our debtors.

And do not lead us into temptation,
but deliver us from the evil one.
For yours is the kingdom and the power and the glory forever.

Amen.

Closing Prayer

Have mercy upon us, O God of peace. Empower us to do your will. Do in us what is pleasing to you, through Jesus Christ. And help us to show mercy, as we have been shown mercy.

We ask this through our Lord Jesus Christ, your Son, who lives and reigns with you and the Holy Spirit, one God, for ever and ever. Amen.

Week 1: Tuesday Evening

Call to Praise

After a time of reflective silence, proclaim:

"Love the Lord your God with all your heart and with all your soul and with all your mind." This is the first and greatest commandment. And the second is like it: "Love your neighbor as yourself." All the Law and the Prophets hang on these two commandments.

Psalm 15

A psalm of David.

Lord, who may be a guest in your home?
Who may live on your holy hill?

Whoever lives a blameless life,
does what is right,
and speaks honestly.

He does not slander,
or do harm to others,
or insult his neighbor.

He despises a reprobate,
but honors the Lord's loyal followers.

He makes firm commitments and does not renege on his promise.
He does not charge interest when he lends his money.

He does not take bribes to testify against the innocent.

The one who lives like this will never be upended.

Matthew 5:8

Blessed are the pure in heart, for they will see God.

1 Peter 1:15-22

But like the Holy One who called you, become holy yourselves in all of your conduct, for it is written, "You shall be holy, because I am holy."

And if you address as Father the one who impartially judges according to each one's work, live out the time of your sojourn in reverence. You know that from your empty way of life inherited from your ancestors you were ransomed—not by perishable things like silver or gold, but by precious blood like that of an unblemished and spotless lamb, namely Christ. He was foreknown before the foundation of the world but was manifested in these last times for your sake. Through him you now trust in God, who raised him from the dead and gave him glory, so that your faith and hope are in God.

You have purified your souls by obeying the truth in order to show sincere mutual love. So love one another earnestly from a pure heart.

1 Peter 2:9-10

But you are a chosen race, a royal priesthood, a holy nation, a people of his own, so that you may proclaim the virtues of the one who called you out of darkness into his marvelous light. You once were not a people, but now you are God's people. You were shown no mercy, but now you have received mercy.

Consider what it means to live as a holy priesthood in an unholy society. Pray for holiness and purity and a deepened reverence for our Holy God.

Zechariah's Song

Blessed be the Lord God of Israel,
because he has come to help and has redeemed his people.

For he has raised up a horn of salvation for us
in the house of his servant David,
as he spoke through the mouth
of his holy prophets from long ago,

that we should be saved from our enemies,
and from the hand of all who hate us.

He has done this to show mercy to our ancestors,
and to remember his holy covenant,

the oath that he swore to our father Abraham.

This oath grants that we,
being rescued from the hand of our enemies,
may serve him without fear,

in holiness and righteousness before him for as long as we live.

And you, child, will be called the prophet of the Most High.
For you will go before the Lord to prepare his ways,

to give his people knowledge of salvation
through the forgiveness of their sins.

Because of our God's tender mercy
the morning star will visit us from on high

to give light to those who sin in darkness
and in the shadow of death,
to guide our feet into the way of peace.

Closing Prayer

Lord, may our love overflow—for one another, and for our
neighbors. Strengthen our hearts so that we will be blameless
and holy when our Lord Jesus comes with all his holy ones.

We ask this through our Lord Jesus Christ, your Son, who lives
and reigns with you and the Holy Spirit, one God, for ever and
ever. Amen.

Week 1: Wednesday Morning

*In the morning, before you begin the day, stand with reverence
before the All-Seeing God and say:*

(+) In the Name of the Father, and of the Son, and of the Holy Spirit. Amen.

Having invoked the Holy Trinity, keep silence for a little while, so that your thoughts and feelings may be freed from worldly cares. Then recite the following prayers without haste, and with your whole heart.

The Tax Collector's Prayer

God, have mercy on me, a sinner.

Opening Prayer

Lord, open our lips and our mouths will proclaim your praise.
You are good to those who wait for you, to all who seek you.

Matthew 5:9

Blessed are the peacemakers, for they will be called the children of God.

John 20:19-23

On the evening of that day, the first day of the week, the disciples had gathered together and locked the doors of where they were because they were afraid of the Jewish leaders. Jesus came and stood among them and said to them, "Peace be with you." When he said this, he showed them his hands and his side. Then the disciples rejoiced when they saw the Lord.

So Jesus said to them again, "Peace be with you. Just as the Father has sent me, I also send you." And after he said this, he breathed on them and said, "Receive the Holy Spirit. If you forgive anyone's sins, they are forgiven; if you retain anyone's sins, they are retained."

After a time of reflection, pray that you may be an agent of God's peace. Ask God to show you the places where he is calling you to bring his peace. Ask God to show you how you may bring his peace to your neighborhood.

The Lord's Prayer

Our Father in heaven,
hallowed be your name,

may your kingdom come,
may your will be done
on earth as it is in heaven.

Give us today our daily bread.

And forgive us our debts,
as we ourselves have forgiven our debtors.

And do not lead us into temptation,
but deliver us from the evil one.
For yours is the kingdom and the power and the glory forever.

Amen.

Closing Prayer

Lord, make us instruments of your peace,
Where there is hatred, let us sow love;
where there is injury, pardon;
where there is doubt, faith;
where there is despair, hope;
where there is darkness, light;
where there is sadness, joy;
O Divine Master,
grant that we may not so much seek
to be consoled as to console;
to be understood as to understand;
to be loved as to love.
For it is in giving that we receive;
it is in pardoning that we are pardoned;
and it is in dying that we are born to eternal life.

We ask this through our Lord Jesus Christ, your Son, who lives and reigns with you and the Holy Spirit, one God, for ever and ever. Amen.

Week 1: Wednesday Evening

Call to Praise

After a time of reflective silence, proclaim:

"Love the Lord your God with all your heart and with all your soul and with all your mind." This is the first and greatest commandment. And the second is like it: "Love your neighbor as yourself." All the Law and the Prophets hang on these two commandments.

Psalm 23

A psalm of David.

The LORD is my shepherd, I lack nothing.

He takes me to lush pastures;
he leads me to refreshing water.

He restores my strength.
He leads me down the right paths
for the sake of his reputation.

Even when I must walk
through the darkest valley,
I fear no danger,
for you are with me;
your rod and your staff reassure me.

You prepare a feast before me
in plain sight of my enemies.
You refresh my head with oil;
my cup is completely full.

Surely your goodness and faithfulness
will pursue me all my days,
and I will live in the Lord's house
for the rest of my life.

Matthew 5:10-12

Blessed are those who are persecuted for righteousness, for the kingdom of heaven belongs to them.

Blessed are you when people insult you and persecute you and say all kinds of evil things about you falsely on account of me.

Rejoice and be glad because your reward is great in heaven, for they persecuted the prophets before you in the same way.

Matthew 10:16-20

I am sending you out like sheep surrounded by wolves, so be as wise as serpents and innocent as doves. Beware of people, because they will hand you over to councils and flog you in the synagogues. And you will be brought before governors and kings because of me, as a witness to them and the Gentiles.

Whenever they hand you over for trial, do not worry about how to speak or what to say, for what you should say will be given to you at that time. For it is not you speaking, but the Spirit of your Father speaking through you.

Pray for opportunities to witness as a sheep among wolves.

Simeon's Song

Now, according to your word, Sovereign Lord,
permit your servant to depart in peace.

For my eyes have seen your salvation,
that you have prepared in the presence of all peoples:

a light, for revelation to the Gentles,
and for glory to your people Israel.

Closing Prayer

We ask for your grace and peace. You are the One who is, and who was, and who is to come. We pray that you will empower us to be your faithful witness, like you Son Jesus Christ, who is the faithful witness, the first born from the dead, and the ruler of the kings of the earth.

We ask this through our Lord Jesus Christ, your Son, who lives and reigns with you and the Holy Spirit, one God, for ever and ever. Amen.

Week 1: Thursday Morning

In the morning, before you begin the day, stand with reverence before the All-Seeing God and say:

(+) In the Name of the Father, and of the Son, and of the Holy Spirit. Amen.

Having invoked the Holy Trinity, keep silence for a little while, so that your thoughts and feelings may be freed from worldly cares. Then recite the following prayers without haste, and with your whole heart.

The Tax Collector's Prayer

God, have mercy on me, a sinner.

Opening Prayer

Lord, open our lips and our mouths will proclaim your praise. You are good to those who wait for you, to all who seek you.

Matthew 5:13-15

You are the salt of the earth. But if salt loses its flavor, how can it be made salty again? It is no longer good for anything except to be thrown out and trampled on by people.

You are the light of the world. A city located on a hill cannot be hidden. People do not light a lamp and put it under a basket but on a lamp stand, and it give light to all in the house. In the same way, let your light shine before people, so that they can see your good deeds and give honor to your Father in heaven.

Ephesians 5:8-16

For you were at one time darkness, but now you are light in the Lord. Walk as children of the light—for the fruit of the light consists in all goodness, righteousness and truth—trying to learn what is pleasing to the Lord. Do not participate in the unfruitful deeds of darkness, but rather expose them! For the things they do in secret are shameful even to mention. But all things being exposed by the light are made evident. For everything made evident is light, and for this reason it says:

> "Awake, O sleeper!
> Rise from the dead,
> and Christ will shine on you!"

Therefore be very careful how you live—not as unwise but as wise, taking advantage of every opportunity, because the days are evil.

Ask the Lord how you can live wisely today—making the most of every opportunity to let your light shine before others.

The Lord's Prayer

Our Father in heaven,
hallowed be your name,

may your kingdom come,
may your will be done
on earth as it is in heaven.

Give us today our daily bread.

And forgive us our debts,
as we ourselves have forgiven our debtors.

And do not lead us into temptation,
but deliver us from the evil one.
For yours is the kingdom and the power and the glory forever.

Amen.

Closing Prayer

Father, help us to be a light in our neighborhood. We ask that you would transform the darkness there into light. We ask that we might share in your ministry of transformation and reconciliation there.

We ask this through our Lord Jesus Christ, your Son, who lives and reigns with you and the Holy Spirit, one God, for ever and ever. Amen.

Week 1: Thursday Evening

Call to Praise

After a time of reflective silence, proclaim:

"Love the Lord your God with all your heart and with all your soul and with all your mind." This is the first and greatest commandment. And the second is like it: "Love your neighbor as yourself." All the Law and the Prophets hang on these two commandments.

Psalm 1

How blessed is the one who does not walk
in the advice of the wicked,
or stand in the pathway with sinners,
or sit in the assembly of scoffers!

Instead, he finds pleasure in obeying the Lord's commands;
he meditates on his commands day and night.

He is like a tree planted by flowing streams;
it yields its fruit at the proper time,
and its leaves never fall off.
He succeeds in everything he attempts.

Not so with the wicked!
Instead, they are like wind-driven chaff

For this reason, the wicked cannot withstand judgment,
nor can sinners join the assembly of the godly.

Certainly the Lord guards the way of the godly,
but the way of the wicked ends in destruction.

Matthew 5:20

For I tell you, unless your righteousness goes beyond that of the scribes and the Pharisees, you will never enter the kingdom of heaven.

Galatians 2:19-21

For through the law I died to the law so that I may live for God. I have been crucified with Christ, and it is no longer I who live, but Christ lives in me. So the life I now live in the body, I live because of the faithfulness of the Son of God, who loved me and gave himself for me. I do not set aside God's grace, because if righteousness could come through the law, then Christ died for nothing!

Meditate upon the faithful love of Christ, and the grace of God. Confess your sins.

Paul's Song

You should have the same attitude toward one another that Christ Jesus had:

Who though he existed in the form of God
did not regard equality with God as something to be grasped,

but emptied himself
by taking on the form of a slave,
by looking like other men,
and by sharing in human nature.

He humbled himself,
by becoming obedient to the point of death—
even death on a cross!

As a result God exalted him
and gave him the name that is above every name,

so that at the name of Jesus every knee will bow,
in heaven and on earth and under the earth,

and every tongue confess that Jesus Christ is Lord
to the glory of God the Father.

Closing Prayer

Father, fill us with your Holy Spirit to help us to love and minister like your Son. We live because of the faithfulness of your Son. May our righteousness surpass that of the scribes and Pharisees as Christ lives in us.

We ask this through our Lord Jesus Christ, your Son, who lives and reigns with you and the Holy Spirit, one God, for ever and ever. Amen.

Week 1: Friday Morning

In the morning, before you begin the day, stand with reverence before the All-Seeing God and say:

(+) In the Name of the Father, and of the Son, and of the Holy Spirit. Amen.

Having invoked the Holy Trinity, keep silence for a little while, so that your thoughts and feelings may be freed from worldly cares. Then recite the following prayers without haste, and with your whole heart.

The Tax Collector's Prayer

God, have mercy on me, a sinner.

Opening Prayer

Lord, open our lips and our mouths will proclaim your praise.
You are good to those who wait for you, to all who seek you.

Matthew 5:21-24

You have heard that it was said to the ancient ones, "Do not murder," and "whoever murders will be subjected to judgment." But I say to you that anyone who is angry with a brother will be subjected to judgment. And whoever says to his brother, "Raca," will be brought before the council, and whoever says, "Fool" will be sent to fiery hell.

So then, if you bring your gift to the altar and there remember that your brother has something against you, leave your gift in front of the altar. First go and be reconciled to your brother and then come and present your gift.

John 15:9-17

Just as the Father has loved me, I have also loved you; remain in my love. If you obey my commandments, you will remain in my love, just as I have obeyed my Father's commandments and remain in his love. I have told you these things so that my joy may be in you, and your joy may be complete. My commandment is this—to love one another just as I have loved you. No on has greater love than this—that one lays down his life for his friends. You are my friends if you do what I command you. I no longer call you slaves, because the slave does not understand what is master is doing. But I have called you friends, because I have revealed to you everything I heard from my Father. You did not choose me, but I chose you and appointed you to go an bear fruit, fruit that remains, so that whatever you ask the Father in my name he will give you. This I command you—to love one another.

Meditate on the love of Christ. Take this time to forgive those who have sinned against you. Release your anger to God as you commit yourself to loving your brothers and sisters.

The Lord's Prayer

Our Father in heaven,
hallowed be your name,

may your kingdom come,
may your will be done
on earth as it is in heaven.

Give us today our daily bread.

And forgive us our debts,
as we ourselves have forgiven our debtors.

And do not lead us into temptation,
but deliver us from the evil one.
For yours is the kingdom and the power and the glory forever.

Amen.

Closing Prayer

Lord, help us to love one another. Live in us and make your love complete in us.

We ask this through our Lord Jesus Christ, your Son, who lives and reigns with you and the Holy Spirit, one God, for ever and ever. Amen.

Call to Praise

After a time of reflective silence, proclaim:

"Love the Lord your God with all your heart and with all your soul and with all your mind." This is the first and greatest commandment. And the second is like it: "Love your neighbor as yourself." All the Law and the Prophets hang on these two commandments.

Psalm 51:1-12

For the music director; a psalm of David, written when Nathan the prophet confronted him after David's affair with Bathsheba

Have mercy on me,
O God, because of your loyal love!
Because of your great compassion,
wipe away my rebellious acts!
Wash away my wrongdoing!
Cleanse me of my sin!

For I am aware of my rebellious acts;
I am forever conscious of my sin.

Against you—you above all—I have sinned;
I have done what is evil in your sight.

So you are just when you confront me;
you are right when you condemn me.

Look, I was guilty of sin from birth,
a sinner the moment my mother conceived me.

Look, you desire integrity in the inner man;
you want me to possess wisdom.

Sprinkle me with water and I will be pure;
wash me and I will be whiter than snow.

Grant me the ultimate joy of being forgiven!
May the bones you crushed rejoice!

Hide your face from my sins!
Wipe away all my guilt!

Create for me a pure heart, O God!
Renew a resolute spirit within me!

Do not reject me!
Do not take your Holy Spirit away from me!

Let me again experience the joy of your deliverance!
Sustain me by giving me the desire to obey!

Matthew 5:27-30

You have heard that it was said, "Do not commit adultery." But I say to you that whoever looks at a woman to desire her has already committed adultery with her in his heart. If your right eye causes you to sin, tear it out and throw it away! It is better to lose one of your members than to have your whole body thrown into hell. If your right hand causes you to sin, cut it off and throw it away! It is better for you to lose one of your members than to have your whole body go into hell.

Colossians 3:5-11

So put to death whatever in your nature belongs to the earth: sexual immorality, impurity, shameful passion, evil desire, and greed which is idolatry. Because of these things the wrath of God is coming on the sons of disobedience. You also lived your lives in this way at one time, when you used to live among them. But now, put off all such things as anger, rage, malice, slander, abusive language from your mouth. Do not lie to one another since you have put off the old man with its practices and have been clothed with the new man that is being renewed in knowledge according to the image of the one who created it. Here there is neither Greek nor Jew, circumcised or uncircumcised, barbarian, Scythian, slave or free, but Christ is all and in all.

Confess your sins to the Lord.

The Song Around the Throne

You are worthy to take the scroll
and to open its seals,
because you were slaughtered,
and at the cost of your own blood you have purchased for God
persons from every tribe and language and people and nation.

You have appointed them as a kingdom
and priests to serve our God,
and they will reign on the earth.

Worthy is the Lamb who was slaughtered
to receive power and wealth and wisdom and strength
and honor and glory and praise!

To the one seated on the throne and to the Lamb
be praise and honor and glory and dominion
forever and ever!

Amen.

Closing Prayer

Lord, forgive our sins; clothe us with compassion, kindness, humility, gentleness, and patience. Above all, help us to love.

We ask this through our Lord Jesus Christ, your Son, who lives and reigns with you and the Holy Spirit, one God, for ever and ever. Amen.

Week 1: Saturday Morning

In the morning, before you begin the day, stand with reverence before the All-Seeing God and say:

(+) In the Name of the Father, and of the Son, and of the Holy Spirit. Amen.

Having invoked the Holy Trinity, keep silence for a little while, so that your thoughts and feelings may be freed from worldly cares. Then recite the following prayers without haste, and with your whole heart.

The Tax Collector's Prayer

God, have mercy on me, a sinner.

Opening Prayer

Lord, open our lips and our mouths will proclaim your praise.
You are good to those who wait for you, to all who seek you.

Matthew 5:38-42

You have heard that it was said, "An eye for an eye and a tooth for a tooth." But I say to you, do not resist an evildoer. But whoever strikes you on the right cheek, turn the other to him as well. And if someone wants to sue you and take your shirt, give him your coat also. And if anyone forces you to go one mile, go with him two. Give to the one who asks you, and do not reject the one who wants to borrow from you.

1 Peter 2:13-17

Be subject to every human institution for the Lord's sake, whether to a king as supreme or to governors as those sent by him to punish wrongdoers and praise those who do good. For God wants you to silence the ignorance of foolish people by doing good. Live as free people, not using your freedom as a pretext for evil, but as God's slaves. Honor all people, love the family of believers, fear God, honor the king.

Ephesians 6:11-12

Clothe yourselves with the full armor of God so that you may be able to stand against the schemes of the devil. For our struggle is not against flesh and blood, but against the rulers, against the powers, against the world rulers of this darkness, against the spiritual forces of evil in the heavens.

Pray for the courage to live as a peacemaker and reconciler. Pray in resistance to the principalities and the powers. Pray that you may live humble lives, submitting to those in power for the Lord's sake.

The Lord's Prayer

Our Father in heaven,
hallowed be your name,

may your kingdom come,
may your will be done
on earth as it is in heaven.

Give us today our daily bread.

And forgive us our debts,
as we ourselves have forgiven our debtors.

And do not lead us into temptation,
but deliver us from the evil one.
For yours is the kingdom and the power and the glory forever.

Amen.

Closing Prayer

Father, may we live as bold citizens of the Kingdom. We pledge our allegiance to you. You are the King! Babylon has fallen! Lord, as we follow you, help us to wage war against our enemy. Father, we know that our enemy is not flesh and blood; let us wage war as you do. Father, you overcome evil with good. Help us to overcome evil with good. You are the Peacemaker. Make us be peacemakers. Help us to turn the other cheek. Help us to resist evil with love.

We ask this through our Lord Jesus Christ, your Son, who lives and reigns with you and the Holy Spirit, one God, for ever and ever. Amen.

Call to Praise

After a time of reflective silence, proclaim:

"Love the Lord your God with all your heart and with all your soul and with all your mind." This is the first and greatest commandment. And the second is like it: "Love your neighbor as yourself." All the Law and the Prophets hang on these two commandments.

Psalm 36

For the music director; written by the Lord's servant, David; an oracle

An evil man is rebellious to the core.
He does not fear God,
for he is too proud
to recognize and give up his sin.

The words he speaks are sinful and deceitful;
he does not care about doing what is wise and right.
He plans ways to sin while he lies in bed;
he is committed to a sinful lifestyle;
he does not reject what is evil.

O Lord, your loyal love reaches to the sky;
your faithfulness to the clouds.
Your justice is like the highest mountains,
your fairness like the deepest sea;
you preserve mankind and the animal kingdom.

How precious is your loyal love, O God!
The human race finds shelter under your wings.
They are filled with food from your house,
and you allow them to drink from the river of your delicacies.
For you are the one who gives and sustains life.

Extend your loyal love to your faithful followers,
and vindicate the morally upright!
Do not let arrogant men overtake me,
or let evil men make me homeless!

I can see the evildoers! They have fallen!
They have been knocked down and are unable to get up!

Matthew 5:43-48

You have heard that it was said, "Love your neighbor" and "hate your enemy." But I say to you, love your enemy and pray for those who persecute you, so that you may be like your Father in heaven, since he causes the sun to rise on the evil and the good, and sends rain on the righteous and the unrighteous. For if you love those who love you, what reward do you have? Even the tax collectors do the same, don't they? And if you greet your brothers, what more do you do? Even the Gentiles do the same, don't they? So then, be perfect, as your heavenly Father is perfect.

Consider your enemies. Pray for them. Pray for those who persecute you. Pray for the people of God around the world. Pray for those who resist the Gospel, especially those in your neighborhood.

The Gloria

Glory to God in the Highest
And peace to His people on earth.
Lord God, heavenly King, Almighty God and Father;
We worship you, we give you thanks,
We praise you for your glory.
Lord Jesus Christ, Only Son of the Father.
Lord God, Lamb of God
You take away the sins of the world, have mercy on us;
You are seated at the right hand of the Father,
Receive our prayer.
For You alone are the Holy One,
You alone are the Lord,
You alone are the Most High Jesus Christ,
With the Holy Spirit in the Glory of God the Father. Amen.

Closing Prayer

Lord, help us to love our enemies in both word and deed. Help us to embody your loving, forgiving, presence in our neighborhood—especially among those who resist the Gospel—especially to those who hate your name.

We ask this through our Lord Jesus Christ, your Son, who lives and reigns with you and the Holy Spirit, one God, for ever and ever. Amen.

week two:
parables from Luke's Gospel

In the morning, before you begin the day, stand with reverence before the All-Seeing God and say:

(+) In the Name of the Father, and of the Son, and of the Holy Spirit. Amen.

Having invoked the Holy Trinity, keep silence for a little while, so that your thoughts and feelings may be freed from worldly cares. Then recite the following prayers without haste, and with your whole heart.

The Tax Collector's Prayer

God, have mercy on me, a sinner.

Opening Prayer

Lord, open our lips and our mouths will proclaim your praise. You are good to those who wait for you, to all who seek you.

Luke 7:36-50

Now one of the Pharisees asked Jesus to have dinner with him, so he went into the Pharisee's house and took his place at the table. Then when a woman of that town, who was a sinner, learned that Jesus was dining at the Pharisee's house, she brought an alabaster jar of perfumed oil. As she stood behind him at his feet, weeping, she began to wet his feet with her tears. She wiped them with her hair, kissed them, and anointed them with the perfumed oil.

Now when the Pharisee who had invited him saw this, he said to himself, "If this man were a prophet, he would know who and what kind of woman this is who is touching him, that she is a sinner."

So Jesus answered him, "Simon, I have something to say to you."

He replied, "Say it, Teacher."

"A certain creditor had two debtors; one owed him five hundred silver coins, and the other fifty. When they could not pay, he canceled the debts of both. Now which of them will love him more?"

Simon answered, "I suppose the one who had the bigger debt canceled."

Jesus said to him, "You have judged rightly."

Then, turning toward the woman, he said to Simon, "Do you see this woman? I entered your house. You gave me no water for my feet, but she has wet my feet with her tears and wiped them with her hair. You gave me no kiss of greeting but from the time I entered she has not stopped kissing my feet. You did not anoint my head with oil, but she has anointed my feet with perfumed oil. Therefore I tell you, her sins, which were many, are forgiven, thus she loved much; but the one who is forgiven little loves little."

Then Jesus said to her, "Your sins are forgiven."

But those who were at the table with him began to say among themselves, "Who is this, who even forgives sins?"

He said to the woman, "Your faith has saved you; go in peace."

Confess your sins to God, thanking him for his loving forgiveness. Ask the Lord to examine your heart. Ask him to reveal any snobbery or prejudice in your heart, confessing your sin as it is revealed.

The Lord's Prayer

Our Father in heaven,
hallowed be your name,

may your kingdom come,
may your will be done
on earth as it is in heaven.

Give us today our daily bread.

And forgive us our debts,
as we ourselves have forgiven our debtors.

And do not lead us into temptation,
but deliver us from the evil one.
For yours is the kingdom and the power and the glory forever.

Amen.

Closing Prayer

O God, may your abundant grace, the reconciling love of Christ, and the indwelling presence of the Spirit make us new creatures, so that as old things pass away all things may become new. May you send us as your ambassadors of reconciliation into the world, and into our neighborhood.

We ask this through our Lord Jesus Christ, your Son, who lives and reigns with you and the Holy Spirit, one God, for ever and ever. Amen.

Week 2: Sunday Evening

Call to Praise

After a time of reflective silence, proclaim:

"Love the Lord your God with all your heart and with all your soul and with all your mind." This is the first and greatest commandment. And the second is like it: "Love your neighbor as yourself." All the Law and the Prophets hang on these two commandments.

Psalm 78:1-8

A well-written song by Asaph.

Pay attention, my people, to my instruction!
Listen to the words I speak!

I will sing a song that imparts wisdom;
I will make insightful observations about the past.

What we have heard and learned—
that which our ancestors have told us—
we will not hide from their descendants.

We will tell the next generation
about the Lord's praiseworthy acts,
about his strength and the amazing things he has done.

He established a rule in Jacob;
he set up a law in Israel.
He commanded our ancestors
to make his deeds known to their descendants,
so that the next generation, children yet to be born,
might know about them.

They will grow up and tell their descendants about them.
Then they will place their confidence in God.
They will not forget the works of God,
and they will obey his commands.

Then they will not be like their ancestors,
who were a stubborn and rebellious generation,
a generation that was not committed
and faithful to God.

Luke 8:5-15

"A sower went out to sow his seed. And as he sowed, some fell along the path and was trampled on, and the wild birds devoured it. Other seed fell on rock, and when it came up, it wither red because it had no moisture. Other seed feel among the thorns, and they grew up with it and choked it. But other seed feel on good soil and grew, and it produced a hundred times as much grain."

As he said this, he called out, "The one who has ears to hear had better listen!"

Then his disciples asked him what this parable meant. He said, "You have been given the opportunity to know the secrets of the kingdom of God, but for others they are in parables, so that 'although they see they may not see, and although they hear they may not understand.'

"Now the parable means this: The seed is the word of God. Those along the path are the ones who have heard; then the devil comes and takes away the word from their hearts, so that they may not believe and be saved. Those on the rock are the ones who receive the word with joy when they hear it, but they have no root. They believe for a while, but in a time of testing fall away. As for the seed that fell among thorns, these are the ones who hear, but as they go on their way they are choked by the worries and riches and pleasures of life, and their fruit does not mature. But as for the seed that landed on good soil, these are the ones who, after hearing the word, cling to it with an honest and good heart, and bear fruit with steadfast endurance."

Silence yourself before the Lord. Ask him to make your heart fertile soil for his word. Confess any resistance to his word. And pray that God would prepare the hearts of those in our neighborhood for his word.

The Jesus Manifesto

With Jesus, we proclaim:

> *The Spirit of the Lord is upon me,*
> *because he has anointed me*
> *to proclaim good news to the poor.*
> *He has sent me to proclaim release to the captives*
> *and the regaining of sight to the blind,*
> *to set free those who are oppressed,*
> *to proclaim the year of the Lord's favor.*

Father, anoint us with your Spirit. As you sent your Son, your Son has sent us; may we embody the presence of your Son in the world, and in our neighborhood. Empower us to live and proclaim your good news in our neighborhood, and in the world.

Closing Prayer

Lord, may your word accomplish all you desire in us. Lord, may your word accomplish all you desire for all the different people who live in our neighborhood. Lord, may your Word accomplish all you desire for your people everywhere.

We ask this through our Lord Jesus Christ, your Son, who lives and reigns with you and the Holy Spirit, one God, for ever and ever. Amen.

Week 2: Monday Morning

In the morning, before you begin the day, stand with reverence before the All-Seeing God and say:

(+) In the Name of the Father, and of the Son, and of the Holy Spirit. Amen.

Having invoked the Holy Trinity, keep silence for a little while, so that your thoughts and feelings may be freed from worldly cares. Then recite the following prayers without haste, and with your whole heart.

The Tax Collector's Prayer

God, have mercy on me, a sinner.

Opening Prayer

Lord, open our lips and our mouths will proclaim your praise. You are good to those who wait for you, to all who seek you.

Luke 10:25-37

Now an expert in religious law stood up to test Jesus, saying, "Teacher what must I do to inherit eternal life?"

He said to him, "What is written in the law? How do you understand it?"

The expert answered, "Love the Lord your God with all your heart, with all your soul, with all your strength, and with all your mind, and love your neighbor as yourself."

Jesus said to him, "You have answered correctly; do this, and you will live."

But the expert, wanting to justify himself, said to Jesus, "And who is my neighbor?"

Jesus replied, "A man was going down from Jerusalem to Jericho, and fell into the hands of robbers, who stripped him, beat him up, and went off, leaving him half dead. Now by chance a priest was going down that road, but when he saw the injured man he passed by on the other side. So too a Levite, when he came up to the place and saw him, passed by on the other side. But a Samaritan who was traveling came to where the injured man was, and when he saw him, he felt compassion for him. He went up to him and bandaged his wounds, pouring oil and wine on them. Then he put him on his own animal, brought him to an inn, and took care of him. The next day he took out two silver coins and gave them to the innkeeper, saying, 'Take care of him, and whatever else you spend, I will repay you when I come back this way.'

"Which of these three do you think became a neighbor to the man who fell into the hands of robbers?"

The expert in religious law said, "The one who showed mercy to him."

Jesus said to him, "Go and do the same."

Think about your neighbors. Ask God to help you love your neighbor—in word and deed.

The Lord's Prayer

Our Father in heaven,
hallowed be your name,

may your kingdom come,
may your will be done
on earth as it is in heaven.

Give us today our daily bread.

And forgive us our debts,
as we ourselves have forgiven our debtors.

And do not lead us into temptation,
but deliver us from the evil one.
For yours is the kingdom and the power and the glory forever.
Amen.

Closing Prayer

Lord, help us to love our neighbors. Forgive us for the times we've avoided people in need. Forgive us for our unloving attitudes. Help us to love, as you love. Help us to embrace all people as our neighbors.

We ask this through our Lord Jesus Christ, your Son, who lives and reigns with you and the Holy Spirit, one God, for ever and ever. Amen.

Week 2: Monday Evening

Call to Praise

After a time of reflective silence, proclaim:

"Love the Lord your God with all your heart and with all your soul and with all your mind." This is the first and greatest commandment. And the second is like it: "Love your neighbor as yourself." All the Law and the Prophets hang on these two commandments.

Psalm 27

By David.

The LORD is my light and my deliverance.
I fear no one!
The LORD protects my life!
I am afraid of no one!

When evil men attack me
to devour my flesh,
when my adversaries and enemies attack me,
they stumble and fall.

Even when an army is deployed against me,
I do not fear.
Even when war is imminent,
I remain confident.

I have asked the Lord for one thing—
this is what I desire!
I want to live in the Lord's house
all the days of my life,
so I can gaze at the splendor of the Lord
and contemplate in his temple.

He will surely give me shelter
in the day of danger;
he will hide me in his home;
he will place me on an inaccessible rocky summit.

Now I will triumph
over my enemies who surround me!
I will offer sacrifices in his dwelling place and shout for joy!
I will sing praises to the Lord!

Hear me, O Lord, when I cry out!
Have mercy on me and answer me!

My heart tells me to pray to you,
and I do pray to you, O Lord.

Do not reject me!
Do not push your servant away in anger!
You are my deliverer!
Do not forsake or abandon me,
O God who vindicates me!

Even if my father and mother abandon me,
the Lord would take me in.

Teach me how you want me to live;
lead me along a level path
because of those who wait to ambush me!

Do not turn me over to my enemies,
for false witnesses who want to destroy me
testify against me.

Where would I be
if I did not believe I would experience
the Lord's favor in the land of the living?

Rely on the Lord!
Be strong and confident!
Rely on the Lord!

Luke 11:5-12

Then he said to them, "Suppose one of you has a friend, and you go to him at midnight and say to him, "Friend, lend me three loaves of bread, because a friend of mine has stopped here while on a journey, and I have nothing to set before him." Then he will reply from inside, "Do not bother me. The door is already shut, and my children and I are in bed. I cannot get up and give you anything." I tell you, even though the man inside will not get up and give him anything because he is his friend, yet because of the first man's sheer persistence he will get up and give him whatever he needs.

"So I tell you: Ask, and it will be given to you; seek, and you will find; knock, and the door will be opened for you. For everyone who asks receives, and the one who seeks, finds, and to the one who knocks, the door will be opened.

"What father among you, if your son asks for a fish, will give him a snake instead of a fish? Or if he asks for an egg, will give him a scorpion?"

Submit your cares and needs to the Lord.

Mary's Song

My soul exalts the Lord,
and my spirit has begun to rejoice in God my Savior,

because he has looked upon
the humble state of his servant.
For from now on all generations will call me blessed,

because He-Who-is-Mighty has done great things for me,
holy is his name.

He is merciful to those who fear him,
from generation to generation.

He has demonstrated power with his arm;
he has scattered those whose pride wells up from the sheer arrogance of their hearts.

He has brought down the mighty from their thrones,
and has lifted up those of lowly position;

he has filled the hungry with good things,
and has sent the rich away empty.

He has helped his servant Israel,
remembering his mercy,

as he promised to our ancestors,
to Abraham and to his descendants forever.

Closing Prayer

Lord, we draw near to you with sincere hearts and in full assurance of faith, having our hearts sprinkled to cleanse us from a guilty conscience, and having our bodies washed with pure water. Sovereign God, fill us with your Holy Spirit and provide us with all good things.

We ask this through our Lord Jesus Christ, your Son, who lives and reigns with you and the Holy Spirit, one God, for ever and ever. Amen.

Week 2: Tuesday Morning

In the morning, before you begin the day, stand with reverence before the All-Seeing God and say:

(+) In the Name of the Father, and of the Son, and of the Holy Spirit. Amen.

Having invoked the Holy Trinity, keep silence for a little while, so that your thoughts and feelings may be freed from worldly cares. Then recite the following prayers without haste, and with your whole heart.

The Tax Collector's Prayer

God, have mercy on me, a sinner.

Opening Prayer

Lord, open our lips and our mouths will proclaim your praise.
You are good to those who wait for you, to all who seek you.

Luke 12:13-21

Then someone from the crowd said to him, "Teacher, tell my brother to divide the inheritance with me."

But Jesus said to him, "Man, who made me a judge or arbitrator between you two?" Then he said to them, "Watch out and guard yourself from all types of greed, because one's life does not consist in the abundance of his possessions."

He then told them a parable: "The land of a certain rich man produced an abundant crop, so he thought to himself, 'What should I do, for I have nowhere to store my crops?' Then he said, 'I will do this: I will tear down my barns and build bigger ones, and there I will store all my grain and my goods. And I will say to myself, "You have plenty of goods stored up for many years; relax, eat, drink, celebrate!"' But God said to him, 'You fool! This very night your life will be demanded back from you, but who will get what you have prepared for yourself?' So it is with the one who stores up riches for himself, but is not rich toward God."

Think about all of your material possessions. Give up your ownership of these possessions to the Lord. Ask God to show you how you may use these things of his for his purposes.

The Lord's Prayer

Our Father in heaven,
hallowed be your name,

may your kingdom come,
may your will be done
on earth as it is in heaven.

Give us today our daily bread.

And forgive us our debts,
as we ourselves have forgiven our debtors.

And do not lead us into temptation,
but deliver us from the evil one.
For yours is the kingdom and the power and the glory forever.

Amen.

Closing Prayer

Father, help us to live simple lives of gracious generosity. Lord, all we have is yours. Purge the greed from our hearts and help us to live lives of sacrifice, using our resources and abilities for the good of those with greater need.

We ask this through our Lord Jesus Christ, your Son, who lives and reigns with you and the Holy Spirit, one God, for ever and ever. Amen.

Week 2: Tuesday Evening

Call to Praise

After a time of reflective silence, proclaim:

"Love the Lord your God with all your heart and with all your soul and with all your mind." This is the first and greatest commandment. And the second is like it: "Love your neighbor as yourself." All the Law and the Prophets hang on these two commandments.

Psalm 119:33-40

Teach me, O Lord, the lifestyle prescribed by your statutes,
so that I might observe it continually.

Give me understanding so that I might observe your law,
and keep it with all my heart.

Guide me in the path of your commands,
for I delight to walk in it.

Give me a desire for your rules,
rather than for wealth gained unjustly.

Turn my eyes away from what is worthless!
Revive me with your word!

Confirm to your servant your promise,
which you made to the one who honors you.

Take away the insults that I dread!
Indeed, your regulations are good.

Look, I long for your precepts.
Revive me with your deliverance!

Luke 12:35-48

"Get dressed for service and keep your lamps burning; be like people waiting for their master to come back from the wedding celebration, so that when he comes and knocks they can immediately open the door for him. Blessed are those slaves whom their master finds alert when he returns! I tell you the truth, he will dress himself to serve, have them take their place at the table, and will come and wait on them! Even if he comes in the second or third watch of the night and finds them alert, blessed are those slaves! But understand this: If the owner of the house had known at what hour the thief was coming, he would not have let his house be broken into. You also must be ready, because the Son of Man will come at an hour when you do not expect him."

Then Peter said, "Lord, are you telling this parable for us or for everyone?"

The Lord replied, "Who then is the faithful and wise manager, whom the master puts in charge of his household servants, to give them their allowance of food at the proper time? Blessed is that slave whom his master finds at work when he returns. I tell you the truth; the master will put him in charge of all his possessions. But if that slave should say to himself, 'My master is delayed in returning,' and he begins to beat the other slaves, both men and women, and to eat, drink, and get drunk, then the master of that slave will come on a day when he does not expect him and at an hour he does not foresee, and will cut him in two, and assign him a place with the unfaithful. That servant who knew his master's will but did not get ready or do what his master asked will receive a severe beating. But the one who did not know his master's will and did things worthy of punishment will receive a light beating. From everyone who has been given much, much will be required, and from the one who has been entrusted with much, even more will be asked."

Ask the Lord to reveal any unfaithfulness in your heart. Ask him to show you if you are being trustworthy with what he has given you. Confess any sin to the Lord. Ask God to increase your faithfulness.

Zechariah's Song

Blessed be the Lord God of Israel,
because he has come to help and has redeemed his people.

For he has raised up a horn of salvation for us
in the house of his servant David,
as he spoke through the mouth
of his holy prophets from long ago,

that we should be saved from our enemies,
and from the hand of all who hate us.

He has done this to show mercy to our ancestors,
and to remember his holy covenant,

the oath that he swore to our father Abraham.

This oath grants that we, being rescued from the hand of our enemies,
may serve him without fear,

in holiness and righteousness before him for as long as we live.

And you, child, will be called the prophet of the Most High.
For you will go before the Lord to prepare his ways,

to give his people knowledge of salvation
through the forgiveness of their sins.

Because of our God's tender mercy
the morning star will visit us from on high

to give light to those who sin in darkness
and in the shadow of death,
to guide our feet into the way of peace.

Closing Prayer

Father, help us to stand firm. Increase our faith, helping us to give ourselves fully to your work, because we know that our labor is not in vain. Strengthen us, so that we will not become weary in doing good.

We ask this through our Lord Jesus Christ, your Son, who lives and reigns with you and the Holy Spirit, one God, for ever and ever. Amen.

Week 2: Wednesday Morning

In the morning, before you begin the day, stand with reverence before the All-Seeing God and say:

(+) In the Name of the Father, and of the Son, and of the Holy Spirit. Amen.

Having invoked the Holy Trinity, keep silence for a little while, so that your thoughts and feelings may be freed from worldly cares. Then recite the following prayers without haste, and with your whole heart.

The Tax Collector's Prayer

God, have mercy on me, a sinner.

Opening Prayer

Lord, open our lips and our mouths will proclaim your praise.
You are good to those who wait for you, to all who seek you.

Luke 13:22-29

Then Jesus traveled throughout towns and villages, teaching and making his way toward Jerusalem. Someone asked him, "Lord, will only a few be saved?"

So he said to them, "Exert every effort to enter through the narrow door, because many, I tell you, will try to enter and will not be able to Once the head of the house gets up and shuts the door, then you will stand outside and start to knock on the door and beg him, 'Lord, let us in!'

"But he will answer you, 'I don't know where you come from.'

"Then you will begin to say, 'We ate and drank in your presence, and you taught in our streets.'

"But he will reply, 'I don't know where you come from. Away from me, all you evildoers!'

"There will be weeping and gnashing of teeth when you see Abraham, Isaac, Jacob, and all the prophets in the kingdom of God but you yourselves thrown out. Then people will come from east and west, and from north and south, and take their places at the banquet table in the kingdom of God."

Matthew 25:31-46

When the Son of Man comes in his glory and all the angels with him, then he will sit on his glorious throne. All the nations will be assembled before him, and he will separate people one from another like a shepherd separates the sheep from the goats. He will put the sheep on his right and the goats on his left.

58

Then the king will say to those on his right, "Come, you who are blessed by my Father, inherit the kingdom prepared for you from the foundation of the world. For I was hungry and you gave me food, I was thirsty and you gave me something to drink, I was a stranger and you invited me in, I was naked and you gave me clothing, I was sick and you took care of me, I was in prison and you visited me."

Then the righteous will answer him, "Lord, when did we see you hungry and feed you, or thirsty and give you something to drink? When did we see you a stranger and invite you in, or naked and clothe you? When did we see you sick or in prison and visit you?"

And the king will answer them, "I tell you the truth, just as you did it for one of the least of these brothers or sisters of mine, you did it for me."

Then he will say to those on his left, "Depart from me, you accursed, into the eternal fire that has been prepared for the devil and his angels! For I was hungry and you gave me nothing to eat, I was thirsty and you gave me nothing to drink. I was a stranger and you did not receive me as a guest, naked and you did not clothe me, sick and in prison and you did not visit me."

Then they too will answer, "Lord, when did we see you hungry or thirsty or a stranger or naked or sick or in prison, and did not give you whatever you needed?"

Then he will answer them, "I tell you the truth, just as you did not do it for one of the least of these, you did not do it for me."

And these will depart into eternal punishment, but the righteous into eternal life.

Pray for the hungry, the thirsty, the needy, the sick, the imprisoned, and the homeless. Pray too for those who don't know and love Jesus Christ, our Lord.

The Lord's Prayer

Our Father in heaven,
hallowed be your name,

may your kingdom come,
may your will be done
on earth as it is in heaven.

Give us today our daily bread.

And forgive us our debts,
as we ourselves have forgiven our debtors.

And do not lead us into temptation,
but deliver us from the evil one.
For yours is the kingdom and the power and the glory forever.

Amen.

Closing Prayer

Make us worthy, Lord, to serve those throughout the world who live and die in poverty or hunger. Give them, through our hands, their daily bread and your love, peace, and joy.

We ask this through our Lord Jesus Christ, your Son, who lives and reigns with you and the Holy Spirit, one God, for ever and ever. Amen.

Week 2: Wednesday Evening

Call to Praise

After a time of reflective silence, proclaim:

"Love the Lord your God with all your heart and with all your soul and with all your mind." This is the first and greatest commandment. And the second is like it: "Love your neighbor as yourself." All the Law and the Prophets hang on these two commandments.

Psalm 81

For the music director; according to the gittith style; by Asaph.

Shout for joy to God, our source of strength!
Shout out to the God of Jacob!

Sing a song and play the tambourine,
the pleasant sounding harp, and the ten-stringed instrument!

Sound the ram's horn on the day of the new moon,
and on the day of the full moon when our festival begins.

For observing the festival is a requirement for Israel;
it is an ordinance given by the God of Jacob.

He decreed it as a regulation in Joseph,
when he attacked the land of Egypt.

I heard a voice I did not recognize.
It said: "I removed the burden from his shoulder;
his hands were released from holding the basket.

In your distress you called out and I rescued you.
I answered you from a dark thundercloud.
I tested you at the waters of Meribah. (Selah)

I said, "Listen, my people!
I will warn you!

O Israel, if only you would obey me!
There must be no other god among you.
You must not worship a foreign god.

I am the Lord, your God,
the one who brought you out of the land of Egypt.
Open your mouth wide and I will fill it!"

But my people did not obey me;
Israel did not submit to me.

I gave them over to their stubborn desires;
they did what seemed right to them.

If only my people would obey me!
If only Israel would keep my commands!

Then I would quickly subdue their enemies,
and attack their adversaries.

May those who hate the Lord cower in fear before him!
May they be permanently humiliated!

I would feed Israel the best wheat,
and would satisfy your appetite with honey from the rocky cliffs.

Luke 14:15-24

When one of those at the meal with Jesus heard this, he said to him, "Blessed is everyone who will feast in the kingdom of God!"

But Jesus said to him, "A man once gave a great banquet and invited many guests. At the time for the banquet he sent his slave to tell those who had been invited, 'Come, because everything is now ready.' But one after another they all began to make excuses. The first said to him, 'I have bought a field, and I must go out and see it. Please excuse me.' Another said, 'I have bought five yoke of oxen, and I am going out to examine them. Please excuse me.' Another said, 'I just got married, and I cannot come.' So the slave came back and reported this to his master.

"Then the master of the household was furious and said to his slave, 'Go out quickly to the streets and alleys of the city, and bring in the poor, the crippled, the blind, and the lame.' Then the slave said, 'Sir, what you instructed has been done, and there is still room.' So the master said to his slave, 'Go out to the highways and country roads and urge people to come in, so that my house will be filled. For I tell you, not one of those individuals who were invited will taste my banquet!'"

Pray for the people of your neighborhood, that they may respond to the Lord's invitation. Ask God to help you become a faithful servant, going to streets and alleys to extend the Lord's invitation to the poor, the crippled, the blind, and the lame.

Simeon's Song

Now, according to your word, Sovereign Lord,
permit your servant to depart in peace.

For my eyes have seen your salvation,
that you have prepared in the presence of all peoples:

a light, for revelation to the Gentles,
and for glory to your people Israel.

Closing Prayer

Thank you for the invitation to the banquet. We thank you for the faithful servants you sent into the world, to share the Gospel with both Jews and Gentiles. Empower us by your Holy Spirit to go to every part of our neighborhood, and the world, extending your invitation to all people—your invitation into eternal life.

We ask this through our Lord Jesus Christ, your Son, who lives and reigns with you and the Holy Spirit, one God, for ever and ever. Amen.

Week 2: Thursday Morning

In the morning, before you begin the day, stand with reverence before the All-Seeing God and say:

(+) In the Name of the Father, and of the Son, and of the Holy Spirit. Amen.

Having invoked the Holy Trinity, keep silence for a little while, so that your thoughts and feelings may be freed from worldly cares. Then recite the following prayers without haste, and with your whole heart.

The Tax Collector's Prayer

God, have mercy on me, a sinner.

Opening Prayer

Lord, open our lips and our mouths will proclaim your praise.
You are good to those who wait for you, to all who seek you.

Luke 15:1-10

Now all the tax collectors and sinners were coming to hear him. But the Pharisees and the experts in the law were complaining, "This man welcomes sinners and eats with them."

So Jesus told them this parable: "Which one of you, if he has a hundred sheep and loses one of them, would not leave the ninety-nine in the open pasture and go look for the one that is lost until he finds it? Then when he has found it, he places it on his shoulders, rejoicing. Returning home, he calls together his friends and neighbors, telling them, 'Rejoice with me, because I have found my sheep that was lost.' I tell you, in the same way there will be more joy in heaven over one sinner who repents than over ninety-nine righteous people who have no need to repent.

"Or what woman, if she has ten silver coins and loses one of them, does not light a lamp, sweep the house, and search thoroughly until she finds it? Then when she has found it, she calls together her friends and neighbors, saying, 'Rejoice with me, for I have found the coin that I had lost.' In the same way, I tell you, there is joy in the presence of God's angels over one sinner who repents."

Pray for those who are lost, those who are ensnared in sin..

The Lord's Prayer

Our Father in heaven,
hallowed be your name,

may your kingdom come,
may your will be done
on earth as it is in heaven.

Give us today our daily bread.

And forgive us our debts,
as we ourselves have forgiven our debtors.

And do not lead us into temptation,
but deliver us from the evil one.
For yours is the kingdom and the power and the glory forever.

Amen.

Closing Prayer

Our God, we ask that we too would be accused of being a friend to sinners. May the seats around our table always be filled with sinners! Shape us into a hospitable people—a welcoming people who are always willing to leave the ninety-nine for the one.

And may we recognize our own sin, and our own need for forgiveness, so that we do not become proud.

We ask this through our Lord Jesus Christ, your Son, who lives and reigns with you and the Holy Spirit, one God, for ever and ever. Amen.

Week 2: Thursday Evening

Call to Praise

After a time of reflective silence, proclaim:

"Love the Lord your God with all your heart and with all your soul and with all your mind." This is the first and greatest commandment. And the second is like it: "Love your neighbor as yourself." All the Law and the Prophets hang on these two commandments.

Psalm 137

By the rivers of Babylon
we sit down and weep
when we remember Zion.

On the poplars in her midst
we hang our harps,

for there our captors ask us to compose songs;
those who mock us demand that we be happy, saying:
"Sing for us a song about Zion!"

How can we sing a song to the Lord
in a foreign land?

If I forget you, O Jerusalem,
may my right hand be crippled!

May my tongue stick to the roof of my mouth,
if I do not remember you,
and do not give Jerusalem priority
over whatever gives me the most joy.

Remember, O Lord, what the Edomites did
on the day Jerusalem fell.

They said, "Tear it down, tear it down,
right to its very foundation!"

O daughter Babylon, soon to be devastated!
How blessed will be the one who repays you
for what you dished out to us!

How blessed will be the one who grabs your babies
and smashes them on a rock!

Luke 15:11-32

Then Jesus said, "A man had two sons. The younger of them said to his father, 'Father, give me the share of the estate that will belong to me.' So he divided his assets between them.

After a few days, the younger son gathered together all he had and left on a journey to a distant country, and there he squandered his wealth with a wild lifestyle. Then after he had spent everything, a severe famine took place in that country, and he began to be in need. So he went and worked for one of the citizens of that country, who sent him to his fields to feed pigs. He was longing to eat the carob pods the pigs were eating, but no one gave him anything.

But when he came to his senses he said, 'How many of my father's hired workers have food enough to spare, but here I am dying from hunger! I will get up and go to my father and say to him, "Father, I have sinned against heaven and against you. I am no longer worthy to be called your son; treat me like one of your hired workers."' So he got up and went to his father.

But while he was still a long way from home his father saw him, and his heart went out to him; he ran and hugged his son and kissed him.

Then his son said to him, 'Father, I have sinned against heaven and against you; I am no longer worthy to be called your son.'

But the father said to his slaves, 'Hurry! Bring the best robe, and put it on him! Put a ring on his finger and sandals on his feet! Bring the fattened calf and kill it! Let us eat and celebrate, because this son of mine was dead, and is alive again—he was lost and is found!' So they began to celebrate.

"Now his older son was in the field. As he came and approached the house, he heard music and dancing. So he called one of the slaves and asked what was happening. The slave replied, 'Your brother has returned, and your father has killed the fattened calf because he got his son back safe and sound.'

But the older son became angry and refused to go in. His father came out and appealed to him, but he answered his father, 'Look! These many years I have worked like a slave for you, and I never disobeyed your commands. Yet you never gave me even a goat so that I could celebrate with my friends! But when this son of yours came back, who has devoured your assets with prostitutes, you killed the fattened calf for him!'

Then the father said to him, 'Son, you are always with me, and everything that belongs to me is yours. It was appropriate to celebrate and be glad, for your brother was dead, and is alive; he was lost and is found.'"

Pray for the prodigals. Pray too for those who resent the prodigals. As Reflecting upon your own sins, repent and seek the Lord's loving forgiveness.

Paul's Song

You should have the same attitude toward one another that Christ Jesus had:

Who though he existed in the form of God
did not regard equality with God as something to be grasped,

but emptied himself
by taking on the form of a slave,
by looking like other men,
and by sharing in human nature.

He humbled himself,
by becoming obedient to the point of death—
even death on a cross!

As a result God exalted him
and gave him the name that is above every name,

so that at the name of Jesus every knee will bow,
in heaven and on earth and under the earth,

and every tongue confess that Jesus Christ is Lord
to the glory of God the Father.

Closing Prayer

Loving Father, we praise you for your forgiveness. May we forgive as you have forgiven. May our arms embrace the prodigals in the name of your Son, Jesus Christ. May we greet those who are far off with your love.

We ask this through our Lord Jesus Christ, your Son, who lives and reigns with you and the Holy Spirit, one God, for ever and ever. Amen.

Week 2: Friday Morning

In the morning, before you begin the day, stand with reverence before the All-Seeing God and say:

(+) In the Name of the Father, and of the Son, and of the Holy Spirit. Amen.

Having invoked the Holy Trinity, keep silence for a little while, so that your thoughts and feelings may be freed from worldly cares. Then recite the following prayers without haste, and with your whole heart.

The Tax Collector's Prayer

God, have mercy on me, a sinner.

Opening Prayer

Lord, open our lips and our mouths will proclaim your praise.
You are good to those who wait for you, to all who seek you.

Luke 16:1-9

Jesus also said to the disciples, "There was a rich man who was informed of accusations that his manager was wasting his assets. So he called the manager in and said to him, 'What is this I hear about you? Turn in the account of your administration, because you can no longer be my manager.'

"Then the manager said to himself, 'What should I do, since my master is taking my position away from me? I'm not strong enough to dig, and I'm too ashamed to beg. I know what to do so that when I am put out of management, people will welcome me into their homes.'

"So he contacted his master's debtors one by one. He asked the first, 'How much do you owe my master?'

"The man replied, 'A hundred measures of olive oil.'

"The manager said to him, 'Take your bill, sit down quickly, and write fifty.'

"Then he said to another, 'And how much do you owe?'

"The second man replied, 'A hundred measures of wheat.'"

"The manager said to him, 'Take your bill, and write eighty.'

"The master commended the dishonest manager because he acted shrewdly. For the people of this world are shrewder in dealing with their contemporaries than the people of light. And I tell you, make friends for yourselves by how you use worldly wealth, so that when it runs out you will be welcomed into the eternal homes."

Pray that you may be generous and shrewd with your resources. Consider how you may wisely use what you have to bless others and build friendships rather than to seek your own benefit.

The Lord's Prayer

Our Father in heaven,
hallowed be your name,

may your kingdom come,
may your will be done
on earth as it is in heaven.

Give us today our daily bread.

And forgive us our debts,
as we ourselves have forgiven our debtors.

And do not lead us into temptation,
but deliver us from the evil one.
For yours is the kingdom and the power and the glory forever.

Amen.

Closing Prayer

Sovereign God, everything we have belongs to you. May we use what we have to bless others and woo people into the Kingdom, rather than for our own comfort and ease. Bless us so that we may bless others. If we do not bless others, take our resources from us and give them to those who will bless others.

We ask this through our Lord Jesus Christ, your Son, who lives and reigns with you and the Holy Spirit, one God, for ever and ever. Amen.

Week 2: Friday Evening

Call to Praise

After a time of reflective silence, proclaim:

"Love the Lord your God with all your heart and with all your soul and with all your mind." This is the first and greatest

commandment. And the second is like it: "Love your neighbor as yourself." All the Law and the Prophets hang on these two commandments.

Psalm 62

For the music director, Jeduthun; a psalm of David.

For God alone I patiently wait;
he is the one who delivers me.

He alone is my protector and deliverer.
He is my refuge; I will not be upended.

How long will you threaten a man?
All of you are murderers,
as dangerous as a leaning wall or an unstable fence.

They spend all their time planning how to bring him down.
They love to use deceit;
they pronounce blessings with their mouths,
but inwardly they utter curses. (Selah)

Patiently wait for God alone, my soul!
For he is the one who gives me confidence.

He alone is my protector and deliverer.
He is my refuge; I will not be upended.

God delivers me and exalts me;
God is my strong protector and my shelter.

Trust in him at all times, you people!
Pour out your hearts before him!
God is our shelter! (Selah)

Men are nothing but a mere breath;
human beings are unreliable.
When they are weighed in the scales,
all of them together are lighter than air.

Do not trust in what you can gain by oppression!

Do not put false confidence in what you can gain by robbery!
If wealth increases, do not become attached to it!

God has declared one principle;
two principles I have heard:
God is strong,
and you, O Lord, demonstrate loyal love.
For you repay men for what they do.

Luke 16:19-31

"There was a rich man who dressed in purple and fine linen and who feasted sumptuously every day. But at his gate lay a poor man named Lazarus whose body was covered with sores, who longed to eat what fell from the rich man's table. In addition, the dogs came and licked his sores.

"Now the poor man died and was carried by the angels to Abraham's side. The rich man also died and was buried. And in hell, as he was in torment, he looked up and saw Abraham far off with Lazarus at his side. So he called out, 'Father Abraham, have mercy on me, and send Lazarus to dip the tip of his finger in water and cool my tongue, because I am in anguish in this fire.'

"But Abraham said, 'Child, remember that in your lifetime you received your good things and Lazarus likewise bad things, but now he is comforted here and you are in anguish. Besides all this, a great chasm has been fixed between us, so that those who want to cross over from here to you cannot do so, and no one can cross from there to us.'

"So the rich man said, 'Then I beg you, father – send Lazarus to my father's house (for I have five brothers) to warn them so that they don't come into this place of torment.'

"But Abraham said, 'They have Moses and the prophets; they must respond to them.'

"Then the rich man said, 'No, father Abraham, but if someone from the dead goes to them, they will repent.'

"He replied to him, 'If they do not respond to Moses and the prophets, they will not be convinced even if someone rises from the dead.'"

Reflect upon what it is that you treasure in this life. Ask God to help you treasure what he treasures.

The Song Around the Throne

You are worthy to take the scroll
and to open its seals,
because you were slaughtered,
and at the cost of your own blood you have purchased for God
persons from every tribe and language and people and nation.

You have appointed them as a kingdom
and priests to serve our God,
and they will reign on the earth.

Worthy is the Lamb who was slaughtered
to receive power and wealth and wisdom and strength
and honor and glory and praise!

To the one seated on the throne and to the Lamb
be praise and honor and glory and dominion
forever and ever! Amen.

Closing Prayer

Compassionate One, give us compassion for the poor around us. Give us compassion for those in our neighborhood. Help us to stop serving ourselves, but to serve others.

We ask this through our Lord Jesus Christ, your Son, who lives and reigns with you and the Holy Spirit, one God, for ever and ever. Amen.

Week 2: Saturday Morning

In the morning, before you begin the day, stand with reverence before the All-Seeing God and say:

(+) In the Name of the Father, and of the Son, and of the Holy Spirit. Amen.

Having invoked the Holy Trinity, keep silence for a little while, so that your thoughts and feelings may be freed from worldly cares. Then recite the following prayers without haste, and with your whole heart.

The Tax Collector's Prayer

God, have mercy on me, a sinner.

Opening Prayer

Lord, open our lips and our mouths will proclaim your praise.
You are good to those who wait for you, to all who seek you.

Luke 18:1-8

Then Jesus told them a parable to show them they should always pray and not lose heart. He said, "In a certain city there was a judge who neither feared God nor respected people. There was also a widow in that city who kept coming to him and saying, 'Give me justice against my adversary.'

"For a while he refused, but later on he said to himself, 'Though I neither fear God nor have regard for people, yet because this widow keeps on bothering me, I will give her justice, or in the end she will wear me out by her unending pleas.'"

And the Lord said, "Listen to what the unrighteous judge says! Won't God give justice to his chosen ones, who cry out to him day and night? Will he delay long to help them? I tell you, he will give them justice speedily. Nevertheless, when the Son of Man comes, will he find faith on earth?"

Bring your prayers to the Lord, with an open heart. Pray that God would bring justice to where there is injustice.

The Lord's Prayer

Our Father in heaven,
hallowed be your name,

may your kingdom come,
may your will be done
on earth as it is in heaven.

Give us today our daily bread.

And forgive us our debts,
as we ourselves have forgiven our debtors.

And do not lead us into temptation,
but deliver us from the evil one.
For yours is the kingdom and the power and the glory forever.

Amen.

Closing Prayer

Father, vindicate us, your people. Our hope is not in vain. Answer our prayers. Give us persistence and patience and hope as we pray for you to make things right in this world.

We ask this through our Lord Jesus Christ, your Son, who lives and reigns with you and the Holy Spirit, one God, for ever and ever. Amen.

Week 2: Saturday Evening

Call to Praise

After a time of reflective silence, proclaim:

"Love the Lord your God with all your heart and with all your soul and with all your mind." This is the first and greatest

commandment. And the second is like it: "Love your neighbor as yourself." All the Law and the Prophets hang on these two commandments.

Psalm 39

For the music director, Jeduthun; a psalm of David.

I decided, "I will watch what I say
and make sure I do not sin with my tongue.
I will put a muzzle over my mouth
while in the presence of an evil man."

I was stone silent;
I held back the urge to speak.
My frustration grew;
my anxiety intensified.

As I thought about it, I became impatient.
Finally I spoke these words:

"O Lord, help me understand my mortality
and the brevity of life!
Let me realize how quickly my life will pass!

Look, you make my days short-lived,
and my life span is nothing from your perspective.
Surely all people, even those who seem secure,
are nothing but vapor.

"Surely people go through life as mere ghosts.
Surely they accumulate worthless wealth
without knowing who will eventually haul it away.

"But now, O Lord, upon what am I relying?
You are my only hope!

Deliver me from all my sins of rebellion!
Do not make me the object of fools' insults!

I am silent and cannot open my mouth
because of what you have done.

Please stop wounding me!
You have almost beaten me to death!

You severely discipline people for their sins;
like a moth you slowly devour their strength.
Surely all people are a mere vapor. (Selah)

"Hear my prayer, O Lord!
Listen to my cry for help!
Do not ignore my sobbing!
For I am dependent on you, like one residing outside his native land;
I am at your mercy, just as all my ancestors were.

Turn your angry gaze away from me, so I can be happy
before I pass away."

Luke 18:9-14

Jesus also told this parable to some who were confident that they were righteous and looked down on everyone else. "Two men went up to the temple to pray, one a Pharisee and the other a tax collector. The Pharisee stood and prayed about himself like this: 'God, I thank you that I am not like other people: extortionists, unrighteous people, adulterers – or even like this tax collector. I fast twice a week; I give a tenth of everything I get.'

"The tax collector, however, stood far off and would not even look up to heaven, but beat his breast and said, 'God, be merciful to me, sinner that I am!'

"I tell you that this man went down to his home justified rather than the Pharisee. For everyone who exalts himself will be humbled, but he who humbles himself will be exalted."

Humble yourself before God. Confess your sins.

The Gloria

Glory to God in the Highest
And peace to His people on earth.
Lord God, heavenly King, Almighty God and Father;
We worship you, we give you thanks,
We praise you for your glory.
Lord Jesus Christ, Only Son of the Father.
Lord God, Lamb of God
You take away the sins of the world, have mercy on us;
You are seated at the right hand of the Father,
Receive our prayer.
For You alone are the Holy One,
You alone are the Lord,
You alone are the Most High Jesus Christ,
With the Holy Spirit in the Glory of God the Father. Amen.

Closing Prayer

God have mercy. Lord Jesus Christ, Son of God, have mercy on us, sinners that we are.

We ask this through our Lord Jesus Christ, your Son, who lives and reigns with you and the Holy Spirit, one God, for ever and ever. Amen.

week three:

Jesus revealed
in John's Gospel

Week 3: Sunday Morning

In the morning, before you begin the day, stand with reverence before the All-Seeing God and say:

(+) In the Name of the Father, and of the Son, and of the Holy Spirit. Amen.

Having invoked the Holy Trinity, keep silence for a little while, so that your thoughts and feelings may be freed from worldly cares. Then recite the following prayers without haste, and with your whole heart.

The Tax Collector's Prayer

God, have mercy on me, a sinner.

Opening Prayer

Lord, open our lips and our mouths will proclaim your praise.
You are good to those who wait for you, to all who seek you.

John 6:35

"I am the bread of life. The one who comes to me will never go hungry, and the one who believes in me will never be thirsty."

Isaiah 55:1-6

"Hey, all who are thirsty, come to the water!
You who have no money, come!
Buy and eat!
Come! Buy wine and milk
without money and without cost!

Why pay money for something that will not nourish you?
Why spend your hard-earned money on something that will not satisfy?
Listen carefully to me and eat what is nourishing!
Enjoy fine food!

Pay attention and come to me!
Listen, so you can live!
Then I will make an unconditional covenantal promise to you,
just like the reliable covenantal promises I made to David.

Look, I made him a witness to nations,
a ruler and commander of nations.

Look, you will summon nations you did not previously know;
nations that did not previously know you will run to you,
because of the Lord your God,
the Holy One of Israel,
for he bestows honor on you."

Seek the LORD while he makes himself available;
call to him while he is nearby!

Revelation 22:17

And the Spirit and the bride say, "Come!" And let the one who
hears say: "Come!" And let the one who is thirsty come; let the
one who wants it take the water of life free of charge.

Seek the Lord, drink deeply of his presence.

The Lord's Prayer

Our Father in heaven,
hallowed be your name,

may your kingdom come,
may your will be done
on earth as it is in heaven.

Give us today our daily bread.

And forgive us our debts,
as we ourselves have forgiven our debtors.

And do not lead us into temptation,
but deliver us from the evil one.
For yours is the kingdom and the power and the glory forever.

Amen.

Closing Prayer

Provider, your grace is sufficient. You satisfy the deep longings our hearts. Nourish our souls. Heal us, transform us, and renew us.

We ask this through our Lord Jesus Christ, your Son, who lives and reigns with you and the Holy Spirit, one God, for ever and ever. Amen.

Week 3: Sunday Evening

Call to Praise

After a time of reflective silence, proclaim:

"Love the Lord your God with all your heart and with all your soul and with all your mind." This is the first and greatest commandment. And the second is like it: "Love your neighbor as yourself." All the Law and the Prophets hang on these two commandments.

Psalm 96

Sing to the Lord a new song!
Sing to the Lord, all the earth!

Sing to the Lord! Praise his name!
Announce every day how he delivers!

Tell the nations about his splendor!
Tell all the nations about his amazing deeds!

For the Lord is great and certainly worthy of praise;
he is more awesome than all gods.

For all the gods of the nations are worthless,
but the Lord made the sky.

Majestic splendor emanates from him;
his sanctuary is firmly established and beautiful.

Ascribe to the Lord, O families of the nations,
ascribe to the Lord splendor and strength!

Ascribe to the Lord the splendor he deserves!
Bring an offering and enter his courts!

Worship the Lord in holy attire!
Tremble before him, all the earth!

Say among the nations, "The Lord reigns!
The world is established, it cannot be moved.
He judges the nations fairly."

Let the sky rejoice, and the earth be happy!
Let the sea and everything in it shout!

Let the fields and everything in them celebrate!
Then let the trees of the forest shout with joy
before the Lord, for he comes!

For he comes to judge the earth!
He judges the world fairly,
and the nations in accordance with his justice.

John 2:1-11

Now on the third day there was a wedding at Cana in Galilee.
Jesus' mother was there, and Jesus and his disciples were also
invited to the wedding. When the wine ran out, Jesus' mother
said to him, "They have no wine left."

Jesus replied, "Woman, why are saying this to me? My time has not yet come."

His mother told the servants, "Whatever he tells you, do it."

Now there were six stone jars there for Jewish ceremonial washing, each holding twenty or thirty gallons. Jesus told the servants, "Fill the jars with water." So they filled them to the very top.

Then he told them, "Now draw some out and take it to the head steward," and they did.

When the head steward tasted the water that had been turned to wine, not knowing where it came from (though the servants who had drawn the water knew), he called the bridegroom and said to him, "Everyone serves the good wine first, and then the cheaper wine when the guests are drunk. You have kept the good wine until now!"

Jesus did this as the first of his miraculous signs, in Cana of Galilee. In this way he revealed his glory, and his disciples believed in him.

Meditate upon this, the first of Jesus' miracles in the Gospel of John. Thank God for new life. Ask him to fill you with his Holy Spirit.

The Jesus Manifesto

With Jesus, we proclaim:

> *The Spirit of the Lord is upon me,*
> *because he has anointed me*
> *to proclaim good news to the poor.*
> *He has sent me to proclaim release to the captives*
> *and the regaining of sight to the blind,*
> *to set free those who are oppressed,*
> *to proclaim the year of the Lord's favor.*

Father, anoint us with your Spirit. As you sent your Son, your Son has sent us; may we embody the presence of your Son in the world, and in our neighborhood. Empower us to live and proclaim your good news in our neighborhood, and in the world.

Closing Prayer

Father, we thank you for revealing yourself to us through your Son, Jesus. We thank you for new life in the new covenant. Remind us of the presence of your Spirit in our midst.

We ask this through our Lord Jesus Christ, your Son, who lives and reigns with you and the Holy Spirit, one God, for ever and ever. Amen.

Week 3: Monday Morning

In the morning, before you begin the day, stand with reverence before the All-Seeing God and say:

(+) In the Name of the Father, and of the Son, and of the Holy Spirit. Amen.

Having invoked the Holy Trinity, keep silence for a little while, so that your thoughts and feelings may be freed from worldly cares. Then recite the following prayers without haste, and with your whole heart.

The Tax Collector's Prayer

God, have mercy on me, a sinner.

Opening Prayer

Lord, open our lips and our mouths will proclaim your praise. You are good to those who wait for you, to all who seek you.

John 8:12

"I am the light of the world. The one who follows me will never walk in darkness, but will have the light of life."

1 Peter 2:9-10

But you are a chosen race, a royal priesthood, a holy nation, a people of his own, so that you may proclaim the virtues of the one who called you out of darkness into his marvelous light. You once were not a people, but now you are God's people. You were shown no mercy, but now you have received mercy.

Reflect upon the darkness out of which you were called. Praise the Lord for the light in which you now live.

The Lord's Prayer

Our Father in heaven,
hallowed be your name,

may your kingdom come,
may your will be done
on earth as it is in heaven.

Give us today our daily bread.

And forgive us our debts,
as we ourselves have forgiven our debtors.

And do not lead us into temptation,
but deliver us from the evil one.
For yours is the kingdom and the power and the glory forever.

Amen.

Closing Prayer

Father, thank you for sending your Son into this world—a light calling us out of darkness. We pray that you would shine your light through us into the lives of the people we meet—especially those in our neighborhood. Call them out of darkness into your light.

We ask this through our Lord Jesus Christ, your Son, who lives and reigns with you and the Holy Spirit, one God, for ever and ever. Amen.

Week 3: Monday Evening

Call to Praise

After a time of reflective silence, proclaim:

"Love the Lord your God with all your heart and with all your soul and with all your mind." This is the first and greatest commandment. And the second is like it: "Love your neighbor as yourself." All the Law and the Prophets hang on these two commandments.

Psalm 77

For the music director, Jeduthun; a psalm of Asaph.

I will cry out to God and call for help!
I will cry out to God and he will pay attention to me.

In my time of trouble I sought the Lord.
I kept my hand raised in prayer throughout the night.
I refused to be comforted.

I said, "I will remember God while I groan;
I will think about him while my strength leaves me." (Selah)

You held my eyelids open;
I was troubled and could not speak.

I thought about the days of old,
about ancient times.

I said, "During the night I will remember the song I once sang;
I will think very carefully."
I tried to make sense of what was happening.

I asked, "Will the Lord reject me forever?
Will he never again show me his favor?

Has his loyal love disappeared forever?
Has his promise failed forever?

Has God forgotten to be merciful?
Has his anger stifled his compassion?"

Then I said, "I am sickened by the thought
that the sovereign One might become inactive.

I will remember the works of the Lord.
Yes, I will remember the amazing things you did long ago!

I will think about all you have done;
I will reflect upon your deeds!"

O God, your deeds are extraordinary!
What god can compare to our great God?

You are the God who does amazing things;
you have revealed your strength among the nations.

You delivered your people by your strength –
the children of Jacob and Joseph. (Selah)

The waters saw you, O God,
the waters saw you and trembled.
Yes, the depths of the sea shook with fear.

The clouds poured down rain;
the skies thundered.
Yes, your arrows flashed about.

Your thunderous voice was heard in the wind;
the lightning bolts lit up the world;
the earth trembled and shook.

You walked through the sea;
you passed through the surging waters,
but left no footprints.

You led your people like a flock of sheep,
by the hand of Moses and Aaron.

John 4:46-51

Now he came again to Cana in Galilee where he had made the water wine. In Capernaum there was a certain royal official whose son was sick. When he heard that Jesus had come back from Judea to Galilee, he went to him and begged him to come down and heal his son, who was about to die.

So Jesus said to him, "Unless you people see signs and wonders you will never believe!"

"Sir," the official said to him, "come down before my child dies."

Jesus told him, "Go home; your son will live."

The man believed the word that Jesus spoke to him, and set off for home. While he was on his way down, his slaves met him and told him that his son was going to live.

Meditate upon this, the second of Jesus' miracles in the Gospel of John. Pray for those who are sick.

Mary's Song

My soul exalts the Lord,
and my spirit has begun to rejoice in God my Savior,

because he has looked upon
the humble state of his servant.
For from now on all generations will call me blessed,

because He-Who-is-Mighty has done great things for me,
holy is his name.

He is merciful to those who fear him,
from generation to generation.

He has demonstrated power with his arm;
he has scattered those whose pride wells up from the sheer
arrogance of their hearts.

He has brought down the mighty from their thrones,
and has lifted up those of lowly position;

he has filled the hungry with good things,
and has sent the rich away empty.

He has helped his servant Israel,
remembering his mercy,

as he promised to our ancestors,
to Abraham and to his descendants forever.

Closing Prayer

Lord, heal us! Lord, heal the ones we love. Though our faith is weak, we cry out to you to bring healing to those we remember now. *Speak the names of those in need of healing.*

We ask this through our Lord Jesus Christ, your Son, who lives and reigns with you and the Holy Spirit, one God, for ever and ever. Amen.

Week 3: Tuesday Morning

In the morning, before you begin the day, stand with reverence before the All-Seeing God and say:

(+) In the Name of the Father, and of the Son, and of the Holy Spirit. Amen.

Having invoked the Holy Trinity, keep silence for a little while, so that your thoughts and feelings may be freed from worldly cares. Then recite the following prayers without haste, and with your whole heart.

The Tax Collector's Prayer

God, have mercy on me, a sinner.

Opening Prayer

Lord, open our lips and our mouths will proclaim your praise.
You are good to those who wait for you, to all who seek you.

John 10:1-10

"I tell you the solemn truth, the one who does not enter the sheepfold by the door, but climbs in some other way, is a thief and a robber. The one who enters by the door is the shepherd of the sheep. The doorkeeper opens the door for him, and the sheep hear his voice. He calls his own sheep by name and leads them out. When he has brought all his own sheep out, he goes ahead of them, and the sheep follow him because they recognize his voice. They will never follow a stranger, but will run away from him, because they do not recognize the stranger's voice." Jesus told them this parable, but they did not understand what he was saying to them.

So Jesus said to them again, "I tell you the solemn truth, I am the door for the sheep. All who came before me were thieves and robbers, but the sheep did not listen to them. I am the door. If anyone enters through me, he will be saved, and will come in and go out, and find pasture. The thief comes only to steal and kill and destroy; I have come so that they may have life, and may have it abundantly.

Praise God for his salvation. Reflect upon the life you have in Jesus Christ, the door into salvation.

The Lord's Prayer

Our Father in heaven,
hallowed be your name,

may your kingdom come,
may your will be done
on earth as it is in heaven.

Give us today our daily bread.

And forgive us our debts,
as we ourselves have forgiven our debtors.

And do not lead us into temptation,
but deliver us from the evil one.
For yours is the kingdom and the power and the glory forever.

Amen.

Closing Prayer

Speak to us, Lord Jesus, that we may hear your voice and be comforted. You provide safety and salvation to your disciples. Give us the faith to listen and the confidence to follow.

We ask this through our Lord Jesus Christ, your Son, who lives and reigns with you and the Holy Spirit, one God, for ever and ever. Amen.

Week 3: Tuesday Evening

Call to Praise

After a time of reflective silence, proclaim:

"Love the Lord your God with all your heart and with all your soul and with all your mind." This is the first and greatest commandment. And the second is like it: "Love your neighbor as yourself." All the Law and the Prophets hang on these two commandments.

Psalm 146

Praise the Lord!
Praise the Lord, O my soul!

I will praise the Lord as long as I live!
I will sing praises to my God as long as I exist!

Do not trust in princes,
or in human beings, who cannot deliver!

Their life's breath departs, they return to the ground;
on that day their plans die.

How blessed is the one whose helper is the God of Jacob,
whose hope is in the Lord his God,

the one who made heaven and earth,
the sea, and all that is in them,
who remains forever faithful,

vindicates the oppressed,
and gives food to the hungry.

The Lord releases the imprisoned.
The Lord gives sight to the blind.
The Lord lifts up all who are bent over.
The Lord loves the godly.

The Lord protects those residing outside their native land;
he lifts up the fatherless and the widow,
but he opposes the wicked.

The Lord rules forever,
your God, O Zion, throughout the generations to come!
Praise the Lord!

John 5:1-9

After this there was a Jewish feast, and Jesus went up to Jerusalem. Now there is in Jerusalem by the Sheep Gate a pool called *Bethzatha* in Aramaic, which has five covered walkways. A great number of sick, blind, lame, and paralyzed people were lying in these walkways. Now a man was there who had been disabled for thirty-eight years. When Jesus saw him lying there and when he realized that the man had been disabled a long time already, he said to him, "Do you want to become well?"

The sick man answered him, "Sir, I have no one to put me into the pool when the water is stirred up. While I am trying to get into the water, someone else goes down there before me."

Jesus said to him, "Stand up! Pick up your mat and walk."

Immediately the man was healed, and he picked up his mat and started walking. (Now that day was a Sabbath.)

Meditate upon this, the third of Jesus' miracles in the Gospel of John. Pray for those in need of healing. Ask God to heal through you—even when it directly challenges the status quo.

Zechariah's Song

Blessed be the Lord God of Israel,
because he has come to help and has redeemed his people.

For he has raised up a horn of salvation for us
in the house of his servant David,
as he spoke through the mouth
of his holy prophets from long ago,

that we should be saved from our enemies,
and from the hand of all who hate us.

He has done this to show mercy to our ancestors,
and to remember his holy covenant,

the oath that he swore to our father Abraham.

This oath grants that we, being rescued from the hand of our enemies,
may serve him without fear,

in holiness and righteousness before him for as long as we live.

And you, child, will be called the prophet of the Most High.
For you will go before the Lord to prepare his ways,

to give his people knowledge of salvation
through the forgiveness of their sins.

Because of our God's tender mercy
the morning star will visit us from on high

to give light to those who sin in darkness
and in the shadow of death,
to guide our feet into the way of peace.

Closing Prayer

Father, help us to bring healing to those with broken bodies and broken spirits. Empower us to show love to the one who seeks and the one who doesn't seek. May we never shrink from demonstrating your compassion, even if it discredits us.

We ask this through our Lord Jesus Christ, your Son, who lives and reigns with you and the Holy Spirit, one God, for ever and ever. Amen.

Week 3: Wednesday Morning

In the morning, before you begin the day, stand with reverence before the All-Seeing God and say:

(+) In the Name of the Father, and of the Son, and of the Holy Spirit. Amen.

Having invoked the Holy Trinity, keep silence for a little while, so that your thoughts and feelings may be freed from worldly cares. Then recite the following prayers without haste, and with your whole heart.

The Tax Collector's Prayer

God, have mercy on me, a sinner.

Opening Prayer

Lord, open our lips and our mouths will proclaim your praise.
You are good to those who wait for you, to all who seek you.

John 10:11-18

"I am the good shepherd. The good shepherd lays down his life
for the sheep. The hired hand, who is not a shepherd and does
not own sheep, sees the wolf coming and abandons the sheep
and runs away. So the wolf attacks the sheep and scatters them.
Because he is a hired hand and is not concerned about the
sheep, he runs away.

"I am the good shepherd. I know my own and my own know me—
just as the Father knows me and I know the Father—and I lay
down my life for the sheep. I have other sheep that do not come
from this sheepfold. I must bring them too, and they will listen
to my voice, so that there will be one flock and one shepherd.
This is why the Father loves me—because I lay down my life, so
that I may take it back again. No one takes it away from me, but
I lay it down of my own free will. I have the authority to lay it
down, and I have the authority to take it back again. This
commandment I received from my Father."

Be silent and listen for the voice of the Good Shepherd.

The Lord's Prayer

Our Father in heaven,
hallowed be your name,

may your kingdom come,
may your will be done
on earth as it is in heaven.

Give us today our daily bread.

And forgive us our debts,
as we ourselves have forgiven our debtors.

And do not lead us into temptation,
but deliver us from the evil one.
For yours is the kingdom and the power and the glory forever.

Amen.

Closing Prayer

Good Shepherd, thank you for laying down your life for us. Lead us. Protect us from danger. Gather the lost sheep of our neighborhood.

We ask this through our Lord Jesus Christ, your Son, who lives and reigns with you and the Holy Spirit, one God, for ever and ever. Amen.

Week 3: Wednesday Evening

Call to Praise

After a time of reflective silence, proclaim:

"Love the Lord your God with all your heart and with all your soul and with all your mind." This is the first and greatest commandment. And the second is like it: "Love your neighbor as yourself." All the Law and the Prophets hang on these two commandments.

Psalm 107:1-9

Give thanks to the Lord, for he is good,
and his loyal love endures!

Let those delivered by the Lord speak out,
those whom he delivered from the power of the enemy,

and gathered from foreign lands,
from east and west,
from north and south.

They wandered through the wilderness on a desert road;
they found no city in which to live.

They were hungry and thirsty;
they fainted from exhaustion.

They cried out to the Lord in their distress;
he delivered them from their troubles.

He led them on a level road,
that they might find a city in which to live.

Let them give thanks to the Lord for his loyal love,
and for the amazing things he has done for people!

For he has satisfied those who thirst,
and those who hunger he has filled with food.

John 6:1-14

After this Jesus went away to the other side of the Sea of Galilee (also called the Sea of Tiberias). A large crowd was following him because they were observing the miraculous signs he was performing on the sick. So Jesus went on up the mountainside and sat down there with his disciples. The Jewish feast of the Passover was near.

Then Jesus, when he looked up and saw that a large crowd was coming to him, said to Philip, "Where can we buy bread so that these people may eat?" (Now Jesus said this to test him, for he knew what he was going to do.)

Philip replied, "Two hundred silver coins worth of bread would not be enough for them, for each one to get a little."

One of Jesus' disciples, Andrew, Simon Peter's brother, said to him, "Here is a boy who has five barley loaves and two fish, but what good are these for so many people?"

Jesus said, "Have the people sit down." (Now there was a lot of grass in that place.) So the men sat down, about five thousand in number. Then Jesus took the loaves, and when he had given thanks, he distributed the bread to those who were seated. He then did the same with the fish, as much as they wanted.

When they were all satisfied, Jesus said to his disciples, "Gather up the broken pieces that are left over, so that nothing is wasted." So they gathered them up and filled twelve baskets with broken pieces from the five barley loaves left over by the people who had eaten.

Now when the people saw the miraculous sign that Jesus performed, they began to say to one another, "This is certainly the Prophet who is to come into the world."

Meditate upon this, the fourth of Jesus' miracles in the Gospel of John. Seek the sustenance of the Lord. Pray for the hungry.

Simeon's Song

Now, according to your word, Sovereign Lord,
permit your servant to depart in peace.

For my eyes have seen your salvation,
that you have prepared in the presence of all peoples:

a light, for revelation to the Gentles,
and for glory to your people Israel.

Closing Prayer

Father, provide for the hungry in our neighborhood—both those with empty hearts and those with empty stomachs. We offer to you everything we have—though we have few resources—for your purposes. Multiply our humble offerings to serve the people of our neighborhood.

We ask this through our Lord Jesus Christ, your Son, who lives and reigns with you and the Holy Spirit, one God, for ever and ever. Amen.

In the morning, before you begin the day, stand with reverence before the All-Seeing God and say:

(+) In the Name of the Father, and of the Son, and of the Holy Spirit. Amen.

Having invoked the Holy Trinity, keep silence for a little while, so that your thoughts and feelings may be freed from worldly cares. Then recite the following prayers without haste, and with your whole heart.

The Tax Collector's Prayer

God, have mercy on me, a sinner.

Opening Prayer

Lord, open our lips and our mouths will proclaim your praise.
You are good to those who wait for you, to all who seek you.

John 11:25-26a

I am the resurrection and the life. The one who believes in me will live even if he dies, and the one who lives and believes in me will never die.

1 Corinthians 15:14-19

And if Christ has not been raised, then our preaching is futile and your faith is empty. Also, we are found to be false witnesses about God, because we have testified against God that he raised Christ from the dead, when in reality he did not raise him, if indeed the dead are not raised. For if the dead are not raised, then not even Christ has been raised. And if Christ has not been raised, your faith is useless; you are still in your sins. Furthermore, those who have fallen asleep in Christ have also perished. For if only in this life we have hope in Christ, we should be pitied more than anyone.

Give thanks for the new life and the resurrection of the dead.

The Lord's Prayer

Our Father in heaven,
hallowed be your name,

may your kingdom come,
may your will be done
on earth as it is in heaven.

Give us today our daily bread.

And forgive us our debts,
as we ourselves have forgiven our debtors.

And do not lead us into temptation,
but deliver us from the evil one.
For yours is the kingdom and the power and the glory forever.

Amen.

Closing Prayer

Father, thank you for the victory you have given us through our Lord Jesus Christ. May we stand firm, unmovable, giving ourselves to the works you've prepare for us. May we hope in the resurrection as we suffer all things in this world for the sake of your Gospel.

We ask this through our Lord Jesus Christ, your Son, who lives and reigns with you and the Holy Spirit, one God, for ever and ever. Amen.

Week 3: Thursday Evening

Call to Praise

After a time of reflective silence, proclaim:

"Love the Lord your God with all your heart and with all your soul and with all your mind." This is the first and greatest

commandment. And the second is like it: "Love your neighbor as yourself." All the Law and the Prophets hang on these two commandments.

Psalm 46

For the music director; by the Korahites; according to the alamoth style; a song.

God is our strong refuge;
he is truly our helper in times of trouble.

For this reason we do not fear when the earth shakes,
and the mountains tumble into the depths of the sea,

when its waves crash and foam,
and the mountains shake before the surging sea. (Selah)

The river's channels bring joy to the city of God,
the special, holy dwelling place of the sovereign One.

God lives within it, it cannot be moved.
God rescues it at the break of dawn.

Nations are in uproar, kingdoms are overthrown.
God gives a shout, the earth dissolves.

The Lord who commands armies is on our side!
The God of Jacob is our protector! (Selah)

Come! Witness the exploits of the Lord,
who brings devastation to the earth!

He brings an end to wars throughout the earth;
he shatters the bow and breaks the spear;
he burns the shields with fire.

He says, "Stop your striving and recognize that I am God!
I will be exalted over the nations! I will be exalted over the earth!"

The Lord who commands armies is on our side!
The God of Jacob is our protector! (Selah)

John 6:16-21

Now when evening came, his disciples went down to the lake, got into a boat, and started to cross the lake to Capernaum. It had already become dark, and Jesus had not yet come to them. By now a strong wind was blowing and the sea was getting rough. Then, when they had rowed about three or four miles, they caught sight of Jesus walking on the lake, approaching the boat, and they were frightened. But he said to them, "It is I. Do not be afraid." Then they wanted to take him into the boat, and immediately the boat came to the land where they had been heading.

Meditate upon this, the fifth of Jesus' miracles in the Gospel of John. Yield your fears to the Lord; trust his ability to overcome all obstacles in your life.

Paul's Song

You should have the same attitude toward one another that Christ Jesus had:

Who though he existed in the form of God
did not regard equality with God as something to be grasped,

but emptied himself
by taking on the form of a slave,
by looking like other men,
and by sharing in human nature.

He humbled himself,
by becoming obedient to the point of death—
even death on a cross!

As a result God exalted him
and gave him the name that is above every name,

so that at the name of Jesus every knee will bow,
in heaven and on earth and under the earth,

and every tongue confess that Jesus Christ is Lord
to the glory of God the Father.

Closing Prayer

Brother Jesus, you alone stretch out the heavens and tread on
the waves of the sea. Protect us and guide us in the midst of
every trial.

We ask this through our Lord Jesus Christ, your Son, who lives
and reigns with you and the Holy Spirit, one God, for ever and
ever. Amen.

Week 3: Friday Morning

*In the morning, before you begin the day, stand with reverence
before the All-Seeing God and say:*

(+) In the Name of the Father, and of the Son, and of the Holy
Spirit. Amen.

*Having invoked the Holy Trinity, keep silence for a little while,
so that your thoughts and feelings may be freed from worldly
cares. Then recite the following prayers without haste, and with
your whole heart.*

The Tax Collector's Prayer

God, have mercy on me, a sinner.

Opening Prayer

Lord, open our lips and our mouths will proclaim your praise.
You are good to those who wait for you, to all who seek you.

John 14:6

I am the way and the truth and the life. No one comes to the Father except through me.

John 17:20-26

"I am not praying only on their behalf, but also on behalf of those who believe in me through their testimony, that they will all be one, just as you, Father, are in me and I am in you. I pray that they will be in us, so that the world will believe that you sent me. The glory you gave to me I have given to them, that they may be one just as we are one—I in them and you in me— that they may be completely one, so that the world will know that you sent me, and you have loved them just as you have loved me.

"Father, I want those you have given me to be with me where I am, so that they can see my glory that you gave me because you loved me before the creation of the world.

Righteous Father, even if the world does not know you, I know you, and these men know that you sent me. I made known your name to them, and I will continue to make it known, so that the love you have loved me with may be in them, and I may be in them."

Reflect upon how Jesus reveals his Father. Dedicate yourself to following Jesus as the Way to the Father.

The Lord's Prayer

Our Father in heaven,
hallowed be your name,

may your kingdom come,
may your will be done
on earth as it is in heaven.

Give us today our daily bread.

And forgive us our debts,
as we ourselves have forgiven our debtors.

And do not lead us into temptation,
but deliver us from the evil one.
For yours is the kingdom and the power and the glory forever.

Amen.

Closing Prayer

Father, with Jesus we ask that you would unite us. Help us to love each other, just as you love your Son and he loves you.

We ask this through our Lord Jesus Christ, your Son, who lives and reigns with you and the Holy Spirit, one God, for ever and ever. Amen.

Week 3: Friday Evening

Call to Praise

After a time of reflective silence, proclaim:

"Love the Lord your God with all your heart and with all your soul and with all your mind." This is the first and greatest commandment. And the second is like it: "Love your neighbor as yourself." All the Law and the Prophets hang on these two commandments.

Psalm 139

For the music director, a psalm of David.

O Lord, you examine me and know.

You know when I sit down and when I get up;
even from far away you understand my motives.

You carefully observe me when I travel or when I lie down to rest;
you are aware of everything I do.

Certainly my tongue does not frame a word
without you, O Lord, being thoroughly aware of it.

You squeeze me in from behind and in front;
you place your hand on me.

Your knowledge is beyond my comprehension;
it is so far beyond me, I am unable to fathom it.

Where can I go to escape your spirit?
Where can I flee to escape your presence?

If I were to ascend to heaven, you would be there.
If I were to sprawl out in Sheol, there you would be.

If I were to fly away on the wings of the dawn,
and settle down on the other side of the sea,

even there your hand would guide me,
your right hand would grab hold of me.

If I were to say, "Certainly the darkness will cover me,
and the light will turn to night all around me,"

even the darkness is not too dark for you to see,
and the night is as bright as day;
darkness and light are the same to you.

Certainly you made my mind and heart;
you wove me together in my mother's womb.

I will give you thanks because your deeds
are awesome and amazing.
You knew me thoroughly;

my bones were not hidden from you,
when I was made in secret
and sewed together in the depths of the earth.

Your eyes saw me when I was inside the womb.
All the days ordained for me
were recorded in your scroll
before one of them came into existence.

How difficult it is for me to fathom your thoughts about me,
O God!
How vast is their sum total!

If I tried to count them,
they would outnumber the grains of sand.
Even if I finished counting them,
I would still have to contend with you.

If only you would kill the wicked, O God!
Get away from me, you violent men!

They rebel against you and act deceitfully;
your enemies lie.

O Lord, do I not hate those who hate you,
and despise those who oppose you?

I absolutely hate them,
they have become my enemies!

Examine me, and probe my thoughts!
Test me, and know my concerns!

See if there is any idolatrous tendency in me,
and lead me in the reliable ancient path!

John 9:1-7

Now as Jesus was passing by, he saw a man who had been blind from birth. His disciples asked him, "Rabbi, who committed the sin that caused him to be born blind, this man or his parents?"

Jesus answered, "Neither this man nor his parents sinned, but he was born blind so that the acts of God may be revealed through what happens to him. We must perform the deeds of the one who sent me as long as it is daytime. Night is coming when no one can work. As long as I am in the world, I am the light of the world."

Having said this, he spat on the ground and made some mud with the saliva. He smeared the mud on the blind man's eyes and said to him, "Go wash in the pool of Siloam" (which is translated "sent"). So the blind man went away and washed, and came back seeing.

Meditate upon this, the sixth of Jesus' miracles in the Gospel of John. Ask God to reveal the hidden prejudices of your heart. Seek the perfect vision of God.

The Song Around the Throne

You are worthy to take the scroll
and to open its seals,
because you were slaughtered,
and at the cost of your own blood you have purchased for God
persons from every tribe and language and people and nation.

You have appointed them as a kingdom
and priests to serve our God,
and they will reign on the earth.

Worthy is the Lamb who was slaughtered
to receive power and wealth and wisdom and strength
and honor and glory and praise!

To the one seated on the throne and to the Lamb
be praise and honor and glory and dominion
forever and ever!

Amen.

Closing Prayer

Open our eyes to see you as you are. We confess our blindness to you. Open the eyes of the spiritually blind people in our neighborhood. Reveal yourself to them. We ask that you'd reveal yourself to them through us.

We ask this through our Lord Jesus Christ, your Son, who lives and reigns with you and the Holy Spirit, one God, for ever and ever. Amen.

Week 3: Saturday Morning

In the morning, before you begin the day, stand with reverence before the All-Seeing God and say:

(+) In the Name of the Father, and of the Son, and of the Holy Spirit. Amen.

Having invoked the Holy Trinity, keep silence for a little while, so that your thoughts and feelings may be freed from worldly cares. Then recite the following prayers without haste, and with your whole heart.

The Tax Collector's Prayer

God, have mercy on me, a sinner.

Opening Prayer

Lord, open our lips and our mouths will proclaim your praise. You are good to those who wait for you, to all who seek you.

John 15:1-8

"I am the true vine and my Father is the gardener. He takes away every branch that does not bear fruit in me. He prunes every branch that bears fruit so that it will bear more fruit. You are clean already because of the word that I have spoken to you. Remain in me, and I will remain in you. Just as the branch cannot bear fruit by itself, unless it remains in the vine, so neither can you unless you remain in me.

"I am the vine; you are the branches. The one who remains in me—and I in him—bears much fruit, because apart from me you can accomplish nothing. If anyone does not remain in me, he is thrown out like a branch, and dries up; and such branches are gathered up and thrown into the fire, and are burned up. If you remain in me and my words remain in you, ask whatever you want, and it will be done for you. My Father is honored by this, that you bear much fruit and show that you are my disciples."

Commit yourself to Jesus. Pray for fruitfulness.

The Lord's Prayer

Our Father in heaven,
hallowed be your name,

may your kingdom come,
may your will be done
on earth as it is in heaven.

Give us today our daily bread.

And forgive us our debts,
as we ourselves have forgiven our debtors.

And do not lead us into temptation,
but deliver us from the evil one.
For yours is the kingdom and the power and the glory forever.

Amen.

Closing Prayer

Lord Jesus, help us to remain in you. On our own we are incapable of bearing fruit. We confess our insufficiency and ask that you would cleanse us and produce fruit in our lives, the Glory of the Father.

We ask this through our Lord Jesus Christ, your Son, who lives and reigns with you and the Holy Spirit, one God, for ever and ever. Amen.

Week 3: Saturday Evening

Call to Praise

After a time of reflective silence, proclaim:

"Love the Lord your God with all your heart and with all your soul and with all your mind." This is the first and greatest commandment. And the second is like it: "Love your neighbor as yourself." All the Law and the Prophets hang on these two commandments.

Psalm 30

A psalm—a song used at the dedication of the temple; by David.

I will praise you, O Lord, for you lifted me up,
and did not allow my enemies to gloat over me.

O Lord my God,
I cried out to you and you healed me.

O Lord, you pulled me up from Sheol;
you rescued me from among those descending into the grave.

Sing to the Lord, you faithful followers of his;
give thanks to his holy name.

For his anger lasts only a brief moment,
and his good favor restores one's life.

One may experience sorrow during the night,
but joy arrives in the morning.

In my self-confidence I said,
"I will never be upended."

O Lord, in your good favor you made me secure.
Then you rejected me and I was terrified.

To you, O Lord, I cried out;
I begged the Lord for mercy:

"What profit is there in taking my life,
in my descending into the Pit?
Can the dust of the grave praise you?
Can it declare your loyalty?

Hear, O Lord, and have mercy on me!
O Lord, deliver me!"

Then you turned my lament into dancing;
you removed my sackcloth and covered me with joy.

So now my heart will sing to you and not be silent;
O Lord my God, I will always give thanks to you.

John 11:17-44

When Jesus arrived, he found that Lazarus had been in the tomb four days already. (Now Bethany was less than two miles from Jerusalem, so many of the Jewish people of the region had come to Martha and Mary to console them over the loss of their brother.) So when Martha heard that Jesus was coming, she went out to meet him, but Mary was sitting in the house. Martha said to Jesus, "Lord, if you had been here, my brother would not have died. But even now I know that whatever you ask from God, God will grant you."

Jesus replied, "Your brother will come back to life again."

Martha said, "I know that he will come back to life again in the resurrection at the last day."

Jesus said to her, "I am the resurrection and the life. The one who believes in me will live even if he dies, and the one who lives and believes in me will never die. Do you believe this?"

She replied, "Yes, Lord, I believe that you are the Christ, the Son of God who comes into the world."

And when she had said this, Martha went and called her sister Mary, saying privately, "The Teacher is here and is asking for you." So when Mary heard this, she got up quickly and went to him. (Now Jesus had not yet entered the village, but was still in the place where Martha had come out to meet him.) Then the people who were with Mary in the house consoling her saw her get up quickly and go out. They followed her, because they thought she was going to the tomb to weep there.

Now when Mary came to the place where Jesus was and saw him, she fell at his feet and said to him, "Lord, if you had been here, my brother would not have died." When Jesus saw her weeping, and the people who had come with her weeping, he was deeply indignant in spirit and greatly distressed.

He asked, "Where have you laid him?"

They replied, "Lord, come and see."

Jesus wept.

Thus the people who had come to mourn said, "Look how much he loved him!"

But some of them said, "This is the man who caused the blind man to see! Couldn't he have done something to keep Lazarus from dying?"

Jesus, intensely moved again, came to the tomb. (Now it was a cave, and a stone was placed across it.) Jesus said, "Take away the stone."

Martha, the sister of the deceased, replied, "Lord, by this time the body will have a bad smell, because he has been buried four days."

Jesus responded, "Didn't I tell you that if you believe, you would see the glory of God?"

So they took away the stone. Jesus looked upward and said, "Father, I thank you that you have listened to me. I knew that you always listen to me, but I said this for the sake of the crowd standing around here, that they may believe that you sent me."

When he had said this, he shouted in a loud voice, "Lazarus, come out!" The one who had died came out, his feet and hands tied up with strips of cloth, and a cloth wrapped around his face.

Jesus said to them, "Unwrap him and let him go."

Meditate upon this, the last of Jesus' miracles in the Gospel of John. Consider the ways in which death has had a hold in your life. Also consider the ways in which Jesus offers new life.

The Gloria

Glory to God in the Highest
And peace to His people on earth.
Lord God, heavenly King, Almighty God and Father;
We worship you, we give you thanks,
We praise you for your glory.
Lord Jesus Christ, Only Son of the Father.
Lord God, Lamb of God
You take away the sins of the world, have mercy on us;
You are seated at the right hand of the Father,
Receive our prayer.
For You alone are the Holy One,
You alone are the Lord,
You alone are the Most High Jesus Christ,
With the Holy Spirit in the Glory of God the Father. Amen.

Closing Prayer

You bring life where there is death, O Lord. We have been wrapped up in sin and death; you have set us free. Fill us with your life-giving Spirit so that we may bring life to places of death.

We ask this through our Lord Jesus Christ, your Son, who lives and reigns with you and the Holy Spirit, one God, for ever and ever. Amen.

week four:

the journey
to the cross
in Mark's Gospel

Week 4: Sunday Morning

In the morning, before you begin the day, stand with reverence before the All-Seeing God and say:

(+) In the Name of the Father, and of the Son, and of the Holy Spirit. Amen.

Having invoked the Holy Trinity, keep silence for a little while, so that your thoughts and feelings may be freed from worldly cares. Then recite the following prayers without haste, and with your whole heart.

The Tax Collector's Prayer

God, have mercy on me, a sinner.

Opening Prayer

Lord, open our lips and our mouths will proclaim your praise.
You are good to those who wait for you, to all who seek you.

Mark 11:1-11

Now as they approached Jerusalem, near Bethphage and Bethany, at the Mount of Olives, Jesus sent two of his disciples and said to them, "Go to the village ahead of you. As soon as you enter it, you will find a colt tied there that has never been ridden. Untie it and bring it here. If anyone says to you, 'Why are you doing this?' say, 'The Lord needs it and will send it back here soon.'"

So they went and found a colt tied at a door, outside in the street, and untied it. Some people standing there said to them, "What are you doing, untying that colt?" They replied as Jesus had told them, and the bystanders let them go. Then they brought the colt to Jesus, threw their cloaks on it, and he sat on it. Many spread their cloaks on the road and others spread branches they had cut in the fields. Both those who went ahead and those who followed kept shouting,

"Hosanna!"
"Blessed is the one who comes in the name of the Lord!"
"Blessed is the coming kingdom of our father David!"
"Hosanna in the highest!"

Then Jesus entered Jerusalem and went to the temple. And after looking around at everything, he went out to Bethany with the twelve since it was already late.

When Jesus entered Jerusalem he was greeted as a King, but the fickle hearts of the people would soon shift Instead of taking the throne of Israel and confronting Rome, he confronted the powers on the Cross. Take this time to pledge your allegiance to Jesus Christ, the King of Kings.

The Lord's Prayer

Our Father in heaven,
hallowed be your name,

may your kingdom come,
may your will be done
on earth as it is in heaven.

Give us today our daily bread.

And forgive us our debts,
as we ourselves have forgiven our debtors.

And do not lead us into temptation,
but deliver us from the evil one.
For yours is the kingdom and the power and the glory forever.

Amen.

Closing Prayer

Jesus, the crowds praised your name when you entered Jerusalem. Like them, we cry Hosanna! And like them we don't see you as you are, but as we want you to be. We confess our lack of faith.

Give us eyes to see, Father.

We ask this through our Lord Jesus Christ, your Son, who lives and reigns with you and the Holy Spirit, one God, for ever and ever. Amen.

Week 4: Sunday Evening

Call to Praise

After a time of reflective silence, proclaim:

"Love the Lord your God with all your heart and with all your soul and with all your mind." This is the first and greatest commandment. And the second is like it: "Love your neighbor as yourself." All the Law and the Prophets hang on these two commandments.

Psalm 50

A psalm by Asaph.

El, God, the Lord speaks,
and summons the earth to come from the east and west.

From Zion, the most beautiful of all places,
God comes in splendor.

Our God approaches and is not silent;
consuming fire goes ahead of him
and all around him a storm rages.

He summons the heavens above, as well as the earth,
so that he might judge his people.

"Assemble my covenant people before,
those who ratified a covenant with me by sacrifice!"

The heavens declare his fairness,
for God is judge. (Selah)

"Listen my people! I am speaking!
Listen Israel! I am accusing you!
I am God, your God!

I am not condemning you because of your sacrifices,
or because of your burnt sacrifices that you continually offer me.

I do not need to take a bull from your household
or goats from your sheepfolds.

For every wild animal in the forest belongs to me,
as well as the cattle that graze on a thousand hills.

I keep track of every bird in the hills,
and the insects of the field are mine.

Even if I were hungry, I would not tell you,
for the world and all it contains belong to me.

Do I eat the flesh of bulls?
Do I drink the blood of goats?

Present to God a thank-offering!
Repay your vows to the sovereign One!

Pray to me when you are in trouble!
I will deliver you, and you will honor me!"

God says this to the evildoer:
"How can you declare my commands,
and talk about my covenant?

For you hate my instruction
and reject my words.

When you see a thief, you join him;
you associate with men who are unfaithful to their wives.

You do damage with words,
and use your tongue to deceive.

You plot against your brother;
and slander the son of your mother.

When you did these things, I was silent,
so you thought I was exactly like you.
But now I will condemn you
and state my case against you!

Carefully consider this, you who reject God!
Otherwise I will rip you to shreds
and no one will be able to rescue you.

Whoever presents a thank-offering honors me.
To whoever obeys my commands,
I will reveal my power to deliver."

Mark 11:12-21

Now the next day, as they went out from Bethany, he was hungry. After noticing in the distance a fig tree with leaves, he went to see if he could find any fruit on it. When he came to it he found nothing but leaves, for it was not the season for figs. He said to it, "May no one ever eat fruit from you again." And his disciples heard it.

Then they came to Jerusalem. Jesus entered the temple area and began to drive out those who were selling and buying in the temple courts. He turned over the tables of the money changers and the chairs of those selling doves, and he would not permit anyone to carry merchandise through the temple courts. Then he began to teach them and said, "Is it not written: 'My house will be called a house of prayer for all nations'? But you have turned it into a den of robbers!"

The chief priests and the experts in the law heard it and they considered how they could assassinate him, for they feared him, because the whole crowd was amazed by his teaching.

When evening came, Jesus and his disciples went out of the city.

In the morning as they passed by, they saw the fig tree withered from the roots. Peter remembered and said to him, "Rabbi, look! The fig tree you cursed has withered."

Reflect upon the injustices done in the name of God. Reflect upon the state of the Bride of Christ.

The Jesus Manifesto

With Jesus, we proclaim:

> *The Spirit of the Lord is upon me,*
> *because he has anointed me*
> *to proclaim good news to the poor.*
> *He has sent me to proclaim release to the captives*
> *and the regaining of sight to the blind,*
> *to set free those who are oppressed,*
> *to proclaim the year of the Lord's favor.*

Father, anoint us with your Spirit. As you sent your Son, your Son has sent us; may we embody the presence of your Son in the world, and in our neighborhood. Empower us to live and proclaim your good news in our neighborhood, and in the world.

Closing Prayer

O Lord, the great and awesome God, who keeps his covenant of love with those who love him and keep his commandments. We are your people. We, the Church, have sinned and turned away from you. We have turned your House of Prayer for All Nations into a Den of Robbers. We repent and ask that you would make us pure and holy.

We ask this through our Lord Jesus Christ, your Son, who lives and reigns with you and the Holy Spirit, one God, for ever and ever. Amen.

In the morning, before you begin the day, stand with reverence before the All-Seeing God and say:

(+) In the Name of the Father, and of the Son, and of the Holy Spirit. Amen.

Having invoked the Holy Trinity, keep silence for a little while, so that your thoughts and feelings may be freed from worldly cares. Then recite the following prayers without haste, and with your whole heart.

The Tax Collector's Prayer

God, have mercy on me, a sinner.

Opening Prayer

Lord, open our lips and our mouths will proclaim your praise.
You are good to those who wait for you, to all who seek you.

Mark 12:13-17

Then they sent some of the Pharisees and Herodians to trap him with his own words. When they came they said to him, "Teacher, we know that you are truthful and do not court anyone's favor, because you show no partiality but teach the way of God in accordance with the truth. Is it right to pay taxes to Caesar or not? Should we pay or shouldn't we?"

But he saw through their hypocrisy and said to them, "Why are you testing me? Bring me a denarius and let me look at it." So they brought one, and he said to them, "Whose image is this, and whose inscription?"

They replied, "Caesar's."

Then Jesus said to them, "Give to Caesar the things that are Caesar's and to God the things that are God's."

And they were utterly amazed at him.

Reflect upon this encounter. As the bearer of God's image, commit yourself and your possessions to him.

The Lord's Prayer

Our Father in heaven,
hallowed be your name,

may your kingdom come,
may your will be done
on earth as it is in heaven.

Give us today our daily bread.

And forgive us our debts,
as we ourselves have forgiven our debtors.

And do not lead us into temptation,
but deliver us from the evil one.
For yours is the kingdom and the power and the glory forever.

Amen.

Closing Prayer

Lord, we are made in your image. Everything we are and have belongs to you. May you always be first in our hearts, in our thoughts, and in our actions. May we follow you in all things as we live in the shadow of Empire.

We ask this through our Lord Jesus Christ, your Son, who lives and reigns with you and the Holy Spirit, one God, for ever and ever. Amen.

Week 4: Monday Evening

Call to Praise

After a time of reflective silence, proclaim:

"Love the Lord your God with all your heart and with all your soul and with all your mind." This is the first and greatest commandment. And the second is like it: "Love your neighbor as yourself." All the Law and the Prophets hang on these two commandments.

Psalm 41

For the music director; a psalm of David.

How blessed is the one who treats the poor properly!
When trouble comes, the Lord delivers him.

May the Lord protect him and save his life!
May he be blessed in the land!
Do not turn him over to his enemies!

The Lord supports him on his sickbed;
you completely heal him from his illness.

As for me, I said:
"O Lord, have mercy on me!
Heal me, for I have sinned against you!

My enemies ask this cruel question about me,
'When will he finally die and be forgotten?'

When someone comes to visit, he pretends to be friendly;
he thinks of ways to defame me,
and when he leaves he slanders me.

All who hate me whisper insults about me to one another;
they plan ways to harm me.

They say, 'An awful disease overwhelms him,
and now that he is bed-ridden he will never recover.'

Even my close friend whom I trusted,
he who shared meals with me, has turned against me.

As for you, O Lord, have mercy on me and raise me up,
so I can pay them back!"

By this I know that you are pleased with me,
for my enemy does not triumph over me.

As for me, you uphold me because of my integrity;
you allow me permanent access to your presence.

The Lord God of Israel deserves praise
in the future and forevermore!

Amen and Amen!

Mark 14:17-26

Then, when it was evening, he came to the house with the twelve. While they were at the table eating, Jesus said, "I tell you the truth, one of you eating with me will betray me."

They were distressed, and one by one said to him, "Surely not I?"

He said to them, "It is one of the twelve, one who dips his hand with me into the bowl. For the Son of Man will go as it is written about him, but woe to that man by whom the Son of Man is betrayed! It would be better for him if he had never been born."

While they were eating, he took bread, and after giving thanks he broke it, gave it to them, and said, "Take it. This is my body."

And after taking the cup and giving thanks, he gave it to them, and they all drank from it.

He said to them, "This is my blood, the blood of the covenant, that is poured out for many. I tell you the truth, I will no longer drink of the fruit of the vine until that day when I drink it new in the kingdom of God."

After singing a hymn, they went out to the Mount of Olives.

Remember Christ's sacrifice. Take time to acknowledge his presence. Confess your sins and betrayals as you receive his forgiveness.

Mary's Song

My soul exalts the Lord,
and my spirit has begun to rejoice in God my Savior,

because he has looked upon
the humble state of his servant.
For from now on all generations will call me blessed,

because He-Who-is-Mighty has done great things for me,
holy is his name.

He is merciful to those who fear him,
from generation to generation.

He has demonstrated power with his arm;
he has scattered those whose pride wells up from the sheer
arrogance of their hearts.

He has brought down the mighty from their thrones,
and has lifted up those of lowly position;

he has filled the hungry with good things,
and has sent the rich away empty.

He has helped his servant Israel,
remembering his mercy,

as he promised to our ancestors,
to Abraham and to his descendants forever.

Closing Prayer

Father, we remember your son. We thank you for his broken body and his shed blood. Forgive our sins. Fill us with hope as we await the consummation of history, the return of Jesus Christ in all of his glory.

We ask this through our Lord Jesus Christ, your Son, who lives and reigns with you and the Holy Spirit, one God, for ever and ever. Amen.

Week 4: Tuesday Morning

In the morning, before you begin the day, stand with reverence before the All-Seeing God and say:

(+) In the Name of the Father, and of the Son, and of the Holy Spirit. Amen.

Having invoked the Holy Trinity, keep silence for a little while, so that your thoughts and feelings may be freed from worldly cares. Then recite the following prayers without haste, and with your whole heart.

The Tax Collector's Prayer

God, have mercy on me, a sinner.

Opening Prayer

Lord, open our lips and our mouths will proclaim your praise.
You are good to those who wait for you, to all who seek you.

Mark 14:32-52

Then they went to a place called Gethsemane, and Jesus said to his disciples, "Sit here while I pray." He took Peter, James, and John with him, and became very troubled and distressed. He said to them, "My soul is deeply grieved, even to the point of death. Remain here and stay alert."

Going a little farther, he threw himself to the ground and prayed that if it were possible the hour would pass from him. He said, "Abba, Father, all things are possible for you. Take this cup away from me. Yet not what I will, but what you will."

Then he came and found them sleeping, and said to Peter, "Simon, are you sleeping? Couldn't you stay awake for one hour? Stay awake and pray that you will not fall into temptation. The spirit is willing, but the flesh is weak."

He went away again and prayed the same thing. When he came again he found them sleeping; they could not keep their eyes open. And they did not know what to tell him.

He came a third time and said to them, "Are you still sleeping and resting? Enough of that! The hour has come. Look, the Son of Man is betrayed into the hands of sinners. Get up, let us go. Look! My betrayer is approaching!"

Right away, while Jesus was still speaking, Judas, one of the twelve, arrived. With him came a crowd armed with swords and clubs, sent by the chief priests and experts in the law and elders. (Now the betrayer had given them a sign, saying, "The one I kiss is the man. Arrest him and lead him away under guard.")

When Judas arrived, he went up to Jesus immediately and said, "Rabbi!" and kissed him. Then they took hold of him and arrested him. One of the bystanders drew his sword and struck the high priest's slave, cutting off his ear.

Jesus said to them, "Have you come with swords and clubs to arrest me like you would an outlaw? Day after day I was with you, teaching in the temple courts, yet you did not arrest me. But this has happened so that the scriptures would be fulfilled." Then all the disciples left him and fled.

A young man was following him, wearing only a linen cloth. They tried to arrest him, but he ran off naked, leaving his linen cloth behind.

Reflect upon Christ's betrayal. His friends failed to stay awake to pray with him, and later deserted him.

The Lord's Prayer

Our Father in heaven,
hallowed be your name,

may your kingdom come,
may your will be done
on earth as it is in heaven.

Give us today our daily bread.

And forgive us our debts,
as we ourselves have forgiven our debtors.

And do not lead us into temptation,
but deliver us from the evil one.
For yours is the kingdom and the power and the glory forever.

Amen.

Closing Prayer

Father, we thank you for sending your Son to struggle and die. We thank you that he is not only like you—fully Divine, but like us—fully human. He has experienced the depth of humanity, including loneliness and pain. May we never desert the lonely. May we be faithful to your Son by being faithful to the broken-hearted.

We ask this through our Lord Jesus Christ, your Son, who lives and reigns with you and the Holy Spirit, one God, for ever and ever. Amen.

Call to Praise

After a time of reflective silence, proclaim:

"Love the Lord your God with all your heart and with all your soul and with all your mind." This is the first and greatest commandment. And the second is like it: "Love your neighbor as yourself." All the Law and the Prophets hang on these two commandments.

Psalm 110

A psalm of David.

Here is the Lord's proclamation to my lord:
"Sit down at my right hand until I make your enemies your footstool!"

The Lord extends your dominion from Zion.
Rule in the midst of your enemies!

Your people willingly follow you when you go into battle.
On the holy hills at sunrise the dew of your youth belongs to you.

The Lord makes this promise on oath and will not revoke it:
"You are an eternal priest after the pattern of Melchizedek."

O sovereign Lord, at your right hand
he strikes down kings in the day he unleashes his anger.
He executes judgment against the nations;
he fills the valleys with corpses;
he shatters their heads over the vast battlefield.

From the stream along the road he drinks;
then he lifts up his head.

Mark 14:53-65

Then they led Jesus to the high priest, and all the chief priests and elders and experts in the law came together. And Peter had followed him from a distance, up to the high priest's courtyard. He was sitting with the guards and warming himself by the fire.

The chief priests and the whole Sanhedrin were looking for evidence against Jesus so that they could put him to death, but they did not find anything. Many gave false testimony against him, but their testimony did not agree.

Some stood up and gave this false testimony against him: "We heard him say, 'I will destroy this temple made with hands and in three days build another not made with hands.'" Yet even on this point their testimony did not agree.

Then the high priest stood up before them and asked Jesus, "Have you no answer? What is this that they are testifying against you?" But he was silent and did not answer. Again the high priest asked him, "Are you the Messiah, the Son of the Blessed One?"

"I am," said Jesus, "and you will see the Son of Man sitting at the right hand of the Power and coming with the clouds of heaven."

Then the high priest tore his clothes and said, "Why do we still need witnesses? You have heard the blasphemy! What is your verdict?"

They all condemned him as deserving death. Then some began to spit on him, and to blindfold him, and to strike him with their fists, saying, "Prophesy!" The guards also took him and beat him.

Jesus willingly suffered injustice. He stood trial so that we might be free. Reflect upon Jesus' great love for you and his great love for all of those who suffer injustice in the world.

Zechariah's Song

Blessed be the Lord God of Israel,
because he has come to help and has redeemed his people.

For he has raised up a horn of salvation for us
in the house of his servant David,
as he spoke through the mouth
of his holy prophets from long ago,

that we should be saved from our enemies,
and from the hand of all who hate us.

He has done this to show mercy to our ancestors,
and to remember his holy covenant,

the oath that he swore to our father Abraham.

This oath grants that we, being rescued from the hand of our
enemies,
may serve him without fear,

in holiness and righteousness before him for as long as we live.

And you, child, will be called the prophet of the Most High.
For you will go before the Lord to prepare his ways,

to give his people knowledge of salvation
through the forgiveness of their sins.

Because of our God's tender mercy
the morning star will visit us from on high

to give light to those who sin in darkness
and in the shadow of death,
to guide our feet into the way of peace.

Closing Prayer

Father, your Son suffered at the hands of ungodly men. Our
Brother was accused by the unrighteous. We ask that you would
help us to stand with the oppressed and the accused as our
Brother has stood with the oppressed and the accused.

We ask this through our Lord Jesus Christ, your Son, who lives and reigns with you and the Holy Spirit, one God, for ever and ever. Amen.

Week 4: Wednesday Morning

In the morning, before you begin the day, stand with reverence before the All-Seeing God and say:

(+) In the Name of the Father, and of the Son, and of the Holy Spirit. Amen.

Having invoked the Holy Trinity, keep silence for a little while, so that your thoughts and feelings may be freed from worldly cares. Then recite the following prayers without haste, and with your whole heart.

The Tax Collector's Prayer

God, have mercy on me, a sinner.

Opening Prayer

Lord, open our lips and our mouths will proclaim your praise.
You are good to those who wait for you, to all who seek you.

Mark 15:1-15

Early in the morning, after forming a plan, the chief priests with the elders and the experts in the law and the whole Sanhedrin tied Jesus up, led him away, and handed him over to Pilate.

So Pilate asked him, "Are you the king of the Jews?"

He replied, "You say so."

Then the chief priests began to accuse him repeatedly. So Pilate asked him again, "Have you nothing to say? See how many charges they are bringing against you!"

But Jesus made no further reply, so that Pilate was amazed.

During the feast it was customary to release one prisoner to the people, whomever they requested. A man named Barabbas was imprisoned with rebels who had committed murder during an insurrection. Then the crowd came up and began to ask Pilate to release a prisoner for them, as was his custom. So Pilate asked them, "Do you want me to release the king of the Jews for you?" (For he knew that the chief priests had handed him over because of envy.)

But the chief priests stirred up the crowd to have him release Barabbas instead. So Pilate spoke to them again, "Then what do you want me to do with the one you call king of the Jews?"

They shouted back, "Crucify him!"

Pilate asked them, "Why? What has he done wrong?"

But they shouted more insistently, "Crucify him!"

Because he wanted to satisfy the crowd, Pilate released Barabbas for them. Then, after he had Jesus flogged, he handed him over to be crucified.

Jesus was silent before Pilate, like a lamb led to the slaughter. Reflect upon Jesus' silence before Pilate.

The Lord's Prayer

Our Father in heaven,
hallowed be your name,

may your kingdom come,
may your will be done
on earth as it is in heaven.

Give us today our daily bread.

And forgive us our debts,
as we ourselves have forgiven our debtors.

And do not lead us into temptation,
but deliver us from the evil one.
For yours is the kingdom and the power and the glory forever.

Amen.

Closing Prayer

You would not defend yourself, Lord Jesus. As you were
sentenced to death, you would not protest. You willingly laid
down your life for us. Thank you.

Father, make us more like your Son. May we have the same
attitude as Christ—looking to the interests of others, putting
others before us, being obedient to death.

We ask this through our Lord Jesus Christ, your Son, who lives
and reigns with you and the Holy Spirit, one God, for ever and
ever. Amen.

Week 4: Wednesday Evening

Call to Praise

After a time of reflective silence, proclaim:

"Love the Lord your God with all your heart and with all your
soul and with all your mind." This is the first and greatest
commandment. And the second is like it: "Love your neighbor as
yourself." All the Law and the Prophets hang on these two
commandments.

Psalm 69:1-15

*For the music director; according to the tune of "Lilies;" by
David.*

Deliver me, O God,
for the water has reached my neck.

I sink into the deep mire
where there is no solid ground;
I am in deep water,
and the current overpowers me.

I am exhausted from shouting for help;
my throat is sore;
my eyes grow tired of looking for my God.

Those who hate me without cause
are more numerous than the hairs of my head.
Those who want to destroy me, my enemies for no reason,
outnumber me.
They make me repay what I did not steal!

O God, you are aware of my foolish sins;
my guilt is not hidden from you.

Let none who rely on you be disgraced because of me,
O sovereign Lord and king!
Let none who seek you be ashamed because of me,
O God of Israel!

For I suffer humiliation for your sake
and am thoroughly disgraced.

My own brothers treat me like a stranger;
they act as if I were a foreigner.

Certainly zeal for your house consumes me;
I endure the insults of those who insult you.

I weep and fast,
which causes others to insult me;

I wear sackcloth
and they ridicule me.

Those who sit at the city gate gossip about me;
drunkards mock me in their songs.

O Lord, may you hear my prayer and be favorably disposed to
me!
O God, because of your great loyal love,
answer me with your faithful deliverance!

Rescue me from the mud!
Don't let me sink!
Deliver me from those who hate me,
from the deep water!

Do not let the current overpower me!
Don't let the deep swallow me up!
Don't let the pit devour me!

Mark 15:16-20

So the soldiers led him into the palace (that is, the governor's
residence) and called together the whole cohort. They put a
purple cloak on him and after braiding a crown of thorns, they
put it on him. They began to salute him: "Hail, king of the
Jews!" Again and again they struck him on the head with a staff
and spit on him. Then they knelt down and paid homage to him.
When they had finished mocking him, they stripped him of the
purple cloak and put his own clothes back on him. Then they led
him away to crucify him.

*Reflect upon the mockery Jesus received by the soldiers. He had
the power to vindicate himself, yet did nothing.*

Simeon's Song

Now, according to your word, Sovereign Lord,
permit your servant to depart in peace.

For my eyes have seen your salvation,
that you have prepared in the presence of all peoples:

a light, for revelation to the Gentles,
and for glory to your people Israel.

Closing Prayer

We adore you, O Christ, and we bless you. By your Cross you have redeemed the world. You endured shame so that we might be redeemed.

Father, help us to live openly and humbly before you and one another. Help us to stand in solidarity with the humble—those who feel shame, those who have been brought low, those who are mistreated.

We ask this through our Lord Jesus Christ, your Son, who lives and reigns with you and the Holy Spirit, one God, for ever and ever. Amen.

Week 4: Thursday Morning

In the morning, before you begin the day, stand with reverence before the All-Seeing God and say:

(+) In the Name of the Father, and of the Son, and of the Holy Spirit. Amen.

Having invoked the Holy Trinity, keep silence for a little while, so that your thoughts and feelings may be freed from worldly cares. Then recite the following prayers without haste, and with your whole heart.

The Tax Collector's Prayer

God, have mercy on me, a sinner.

Opening Prayer

Lord, open our lips and our mouths will proclaim your praise.
You are good to those who wait for you, to all who seek you.

Mark 15:21-24

The soldiers forced a passerby to carry his cross, Simon of Cyrene, who was coming in from the country (he was the father of Alexander and Rufus). They brought Jesus to a place called Golgotha (which is translated, "Place of the Skull"). They offered him wine mixed with myrrh, but he did not take it. Then they crucified him and divided his clothes, throwing dice for them, to decide what each would take.

Like Simon, we are called to share in Jesus' shame. Reflect upon this. Reflect upon all those that have gone before who have suffered because of their allegiance to Jesus Christ.

The Lord's Prayer

Our Father in heaven,
hallowed be your name,
may your kingdom come,
may your will be done
on earth as it is in heaven.

Give us today our daily bread.

And forgive us our debts,
as we ourselves have forgiven our debtors.

And do not lead us into temptation,
but deliver us from the evil one.
For yours is the kingdom and the power and the glory forever.

Amen.

Closing Prayer

Lord Jesus, Crucified, have mercy on us! You were made naked so that we might be clothed with righteousness!

Father, give us the faith to take up our cross and follow your Son, Jesus Christ, Our Lord.

We ask this through our Lord Jesus Christ, your Son, who lives and reigns with you and the Holy Spirit, one God, for ever and ever. Amen.

Week 4: Thursday Evening

Call to Praise

After a time of reflective silence, proclaim:

"Love the Lord your God with all your heart and with all your soul and with all your mind." This is the first and greatest commandment. And the second is like it: "Love your neighbor as yourself." All the Law and the Prophets hang on these two commandments.

Psalm 22:1-8

For the music director; according to the tune "Morning Doe;" a psalm of David.

My God, my God, why have you abandoned me?
I groan in prayer, but help seems far away.

My God, I cry out during the day,
but you do not answer,
and during the night my prayers do not let up.

You are holy;
you sit as king receiving the praises of Israel.

In you our ancestors trusted;
they trusted in you and you rescued them.

To you they cried out, and they were saved;
in you they trusted and they were not disappointed.

But I am a worm, not a man;
people insult me and despise me.

All who see me taunt me;
they mock me and shake their heads.

They say, "Commit yourself to the Lord!
Let the Lord rescue him!
Let the Lord deliver him, for he delights in him."

Mark 15:25-32

It was nine o'clock in the morning when they crucified him. The inscription of the charge against him read, "The king of the Jews." And they crucified two outlaws with him, one on his right and one on his left. Those who passed by defamed him, shaking their heads and saying, "Aha! You who can destroy the temple and rebuild it in three days, save yourself and come down from the cross!"

In the same way even the chief priests—together with the experts in the law—were mocking him among themselves: "He saved others, but he cannot save himself! Let the Christ, the king of Israel, come down from the cross now, that we may see and believe!" Those who were crucified with him also spoke abusively to him.

Reflect upon the love of Jesus Christ, who forgave his enemies even while they crucified and mocked him. Pray for patient love. Pray for your enemies.

Paul's Song

You should have the same attitude toward one another that Christ Jesus had:

Who though he existed in the form of God
did not regard equality with God as something to be grasped,

but emptied himself
by taking on the form of a slave,
by looking like other men,
and by sharing in human nature.

He humbled himself,
by becoming obedient to the point of death—
even death on a cross!

As a result God exalted him
and gave him the name that is above every name,

so that at the name of Jesus every knee will bow,
in heaven and on earth and under the earth,

and every tongue confess that Jesus Christ is Lord
to the glory of God the Father.

Closing Prayer

Sovereign God, teach us to keep our arms ever open to love, to forgive and to serve. May we be willing to be hurt rather than hurt, willing to love, even if we are not loved in return.

We ask this through our Lord Jesus Christ, your Son, who lives and reigns with you and the Holy Spirit, one God, for ever and ever. Amen.

Week 4: Friday Morning

In the morning, before you begin the day, stand with reverence before the All-Seeing God and say:

(+) In the Name of the Father, and of the Son, and of the Holy Spirit. Amen.

Having invoked the Holy Trinity, keep silence for a little while, so that your thoughts and feelings may be freed from worldly cares. Then recite the following prayers without haste, and with your whole heart.

The Tax Collector's Prayer

God, have mercy on me, a sinner.

Opening Prayer

Lord, open our lips and our mouths will proclaim your praise.
You are good to those who wait for you, to all who seek you.

Mark 15:33-37

Now when it was noon, darkness came over the whole land until three in the afternoon. Around three in the afternoon Jesus cried out with a loud voice, *"Eloi, Eloi, lema sabachthani?"* which means "My God, my God, why have you forsaken me?"

When some of the bystanders heard it they said, "Listen, he is calling for Elijah!"

Then someone ran, filled a sponge with sour wine, put it on a stick, and gave it to him to drink, saying, "Leave him alone! Let's see if Elijah will come to take him down!"

But Jesus cried out with a loud voice and breathed his last.

Reflect upon the moment when Jesus Christ felt forsaken and utterly alone. Reflect upon the moment when Jesus breathed his last—when he embraced death, so that we might have eternal life.

The Lord's Prayer

Our Father in heaven,
hallowed be your name,

may your kingdom come,
may your will be done
on earth as it is in heaven.

Give us today our daily bread.

And forgive us our debts,
as we ourselves have forgiven our debtors.

And do not lead us into temptation,
but deliver us from the evil one.
For yours is the kingdom and the power and the glory forever.

Amen.

Closing Prayer

Jesus, we deserve, because of our sins, a terrible death. But your death is our hope. May we embrace your cross, burning with love for you, no matter what it costs.

Father, help us to stand in solidarity with the forsaken. Give us the courage and faith to lay down our lives for others, as your Son laid down his life for us.

We ask this through our Lord Jesus Christ, your Son, who lives and reigns with you and the Holy Spirit, one God, for ever and ever. Amen.

Week 4: Friday Evening

Call to Praise

After a time of reflective silence, proclaim:

"Love the Lord your God with all your heart and with all your soul and with all your mind." This is the first and greatest commandment. And the second is like it: "Love your neighbor as yourself." All the Law and the Prophets hang on these two commandments.

Psalm 31:1-16

For the music director; a psalm of David.

In you, O Lord, I have taken shelter!
Never let me be humiliated!
Vindicate me by rescuing me!

Listen to me!
Quickly deliver me!
Be my protector and refuge,
a stronghold where I can be safe!

For you are my high ridge and my stronghold;
for the sake of your own reputation you lead me and guide me.

You will free me from the net they hid for me,
for you are my place of refuge.

Into your hand I entrust my spirit;
you will rescue me, O Lord, the faithful God.

I hate those who serve worthless idols,
but I trust in the Lord.

I will be happy and rejoice in your faithfulness,
because you notice my pain
and you are aware of how distressed I am.

You do not deliver me over to the power of the enemy;
you enable me to stand in a wide open place.

Have mercy on me, for I am in distress!
My eyes are swollen from suffering.
I have lost my strength.

For my life nears its end in pain;
my years draw to a close as I groan.
My strength fails me because of my sin,
and my bones become brittle.

Because of all my enemies, people disdain me;
my neighbors are appalled by my suffering.
Those who know me are horrified by my condition;
those who see me in the street run away from me.

I am forgotten, like a dead man no one thinks about;
I am regarded as worthless, like a broken jar.

For I hear what so many are saying,
the terrifying news that comes from every direction.

When they plot together against me,
they figure out how they can take my life.

But I trust in you, O Lord!
I declare, "You are my God!"

You determine my destiny!
Rescue me from the power of my enemies and those who chase
me.

Smile on your servant!
Deliver me because of your faithfulness!

Mark 15:37-41

But Jesus cried out with a loud voice and breathed his last.

And the temple curtain was torn in two, from top to bottom.
Now when the centurion, who stood in front of him, saw how he
died, he said, "Truly this man was God's Son!"

There were also women, watching from a distance. Among them
were Mary Magdalene, and Mary the mother of James the
younger and of Joses, and Salome. When he was in Galilee, they
had followed him and given him support. Many other women who
had come up with him to Jerusalem were there too.

*The curtain of the temple has been torn in two; we are no
longer separated from God! We are no longer separated from
one another. Seek reconciliation where relationships have been
broken. Pray that those in your neighborhood might be
reconciled to God and one another.*

The Song Around the Throne

You are worthy to take the scroll
and to open its seals,
because you were slaughtered,
and at the cost of your own blood you have purchased for God
persons from every tribe and language and people and nation.

You have appointed them as a kingdom
and priests to serve our God,
and they will reign on the earth.

Worthy is the Lamb who was slaughtered
to receive power and wealth and wisdom and strength
and honor and glory and praise!

To the one seated on the throne and to the Lamb
be praise and honor and glory and dominion
forever and ever!

Amen.

Closing Prayer

Father, you have removed the barrier. You have called us to enter into your presence without fear or shame. Help us to enter boldly! Though we were once strangers, we are now members of your household. Where we were once many peoples, we are now one people. Reconcile the people of our neighborhood to you and to one another. May they be adopted into our family.

We ask this through our Lord Jesus Christ, your Son, who lives and reigns with you and the Holy Spirit, one God, for ever and ever. Amen.

Week 4: Saturday Morning

In the morning, before you begin the day, stand with reverence before the All-Seeing God and say:

(+) In the Name of the Father, and of the Son, and of the Holy Spirit. Amen.

Having invoked the Holy Trinity, keep silence for a little while, so that your thoughts and feelings may be freed from worldly cares. Then recite the following prayers without haste, and with your whole heart.

The Tax Collector's Prayer

God, have mercy on me, a sinner.

Opening Prayer

Lord, open our lips and our mouths will proclaim your praise.
You are good to those who wait for you, to all who seek you.

Mark 15:42-47

Now when evening had already come, since it was the day of preparation (that is, the day before the Sabbath), Joseph of Arimathea, a highly regarded member of the council, who was himself waiting for the kingdom of God, went boldly to Pilate and asked for the body of Jesus. Pilate was surprised that he was already dead. He called the centurion and asked him if he had been dead for some time. When Pilate was informed by the centurion, he gave the body to Joseph. After Joseph bought a linen cloth and took down the body, he wrapped it in the linen and placed it in a tomb cut out of the rock. Then he rolled a stone across the entrance of the tomb. Mary Magdalene and Mary the mother of Joses saw where the body was placed.

Reflect upon the hopelessness of Jesus' friends and family. If you feel hopeless or sorrowful, share it with the Lord.

The Lord's Prayer

Our Father in heaven,
hallowed be your name,

may your kingdom come,
may your will be done
on earth as it is in heaven.

Give us today our daily bread.

And forgive us our debts,
as we ourselves have forgiven our debtors.

And do not lead us into temptation,
but deliver us from the evil one.
For yours is the kingdom and the power and the glory forever.
Amen.

Closing Prayer

Father, give us hope when we are despairing. Bring joy in the midst of our sorrow. Do not leave us in our struggles. Do not leave us without hope.

We ask this through our Lord Jesus Christ, your Son, who lives and reigns with you and the Holy Spirit, one God, for ever and ever. Amen.

Week 4: Saturday Evening

Call to Praise

After a time of reflective silence, proclaim:

"Love the Lord your God with all your heart and with all your soul and with all your mind." This is the first and greatest commandment. And the second is like it: "Love your neighbor as yourself." All the Law and the Prophets hang on these two commandments.

Psalm 40

For the music director; by David, a psalm.

I waited patiently on the Lord,
and he turned toward me
and heard my cry for help.

He lifted me out of the watery pit,
out of the slimy mud.
He placed my feet on a rock
and gave me secure footing.

And he placed in my mouth a new song, praise to our God.
May many see what God has done,
so that they might swear allegiance to him and trust in the Lord!

How blessed is the one who trusts in the Lord
and does not seek help from the proud or from liars!

O Lord, my God, you have accomplished many things;
you have done amazing things
and carried out your purposes for us.
No one can thwart you!
I want to declare them and talk about them,
but they are too numerous to recount!

Receiving sacrifices and offerings are not your desire.
You make that quite clear to me!
You do not ask for burnt sacrifices and sin offerings.

Then I say,
"Look! I come!
What is written in the scroll pertains to me.

I want to do what pleases you, my God.
Your law dominates my thoughts."

I have told the great assembly about your justice.
Look! I spare no words!
O Lord, you know this is true.

I have not failed to tell about your justice;
I spoke about your reliability and deliverance;
I have not neglected to tell the great assembly about your loyal
love and faithfulness.

O Lord, you do not withhold your compassion from me.
May your loyal love and faithfulness continually protect me!

For innumerable dangers surround me.
My sins overtake me
so I am unable to see;
they outnumber the hairs of my head
so my strength fails me.

Please be willing, O Lord, to rescue me!
O Lord, hurry and help me!

May those who are trying to snatch away my life
be totally embarrassed and ashamed!
May those who want to harm me
be turned back and ashamed!

May those who say to me, "Aha! Aha!"
be humiliated and disgraced!

May all those who seek you be happy and rejoice in you!
May those who love to experience your deliverance say
continually, "May the Lord be praised!"

I am oppressed and needy!
May the Lord pay attention to me!
You are my helper and my deliverer!
O my God, do not delay!

Mark 16:1-8

When the Sabbath was over, Mary Magdalene, Mary the mother
of James, and Salome bought aromatic spices[1] so that they might
go and anoint him. And very early on the first day of the week,
at sunrise, they went to the tomb. They had been asking each
other, "Who will roll away the stone for us from the entrance to
the tomb?"

But when they looked up, they saw that the stone, which was
very large, had been rolled back. Then as they went into the
tomb, they saw a young man dressed in a white robe sitting on
the right side; and they were alarmed.

But he said to them, "Do not be alarmed. You are looking for
Jesus the Nazarene, who was crucified. He has been raised! He is
not here. Look, there is the place where they laid him. But go,
tell his disciples, even Peter, that he is going ahead of you into
Galilee. You will see him there, just as he told you."

Then they went out and ran from the tomb, for terror and
bewilderment had seized them. And they said nothing to anyone,
because they were afraid.

Jesus has triumphed over sin and death. He has triumphed over evil. He has risen, and he lives now and forever. Ask Jesus to reveal himself to you know, the Living One who is ever-present through his Holy Spirit.

The Gloria

Glory to God in the Highest
And peace to His people on earth.
Lord God, heavenly King, Almighty God and Father;
We worship you, we give you thanks,
We praise you for your glory.
Lord Jesus Christ, Only Son of the Father.
Lord God, Lamb of God
You take away the sins of the world, have mercy on us;
You are seated at the right hand of the Father,
Receive our prayer.
For You alone are the Holy One,
You alone are the Lord,
You alone are the Most High Jesus Christ,
With the Holy Spirit in the Glory of God the Father. Amen.

Closing Prayer

Father, may we live and proclaim the Good News of your Son's death and resurrection. Your Son lives and reigns with you, and he is still present among us by your Holy Spirit. May we never take this truth for granted.

We want to know Christ, to know the power of his resurrection and participation in his sufferings, becoming like him in his death, and so, somehow, attaining to the resurrection from the dead.

We ask this through our Lord Jesus Christ, your Son, who lives and reigns with you and the Holy Spirit, one God, for ever and ever. Amen.

+ + +

The Missio Dei Rule of Faith

Missio Dei is a community of people committed to following Jesus' way of peace, simplicity, prayer, and hospitality.

Missio Dei lives to embody Jesus' presence—particularly on the West Bank. The West Bank is a diverse neighborhood of immigrants and punks and artists and homeless people and students and professionals.

Missio Dei is a missional order. We are missional in that we are a part of God's mission on the West Bank. We don't wait for people to come to us, we are committed to going to the people wherever they are. We are an order in that we share core spiritual practices. The rhythm of these practices gives structure to our life together.

Living our life with God, in the way of Jesus, by the empowerment of the Spirit, and in affirmation of the Nicene Creed (381AD) and Apostle's Creed, we are committed to the following:

We are committed to centering our lives on Jesus Christ.

+ We will devote ourselves to a careful reading of the Gospel, going from Gospel to life and life to Gospel.

+ We will actively seek to encounter the living and active person of Jesus Christ through the reading of Scripture and through prayer, trusting in the power of the Holy Spirit to shape us into the likeness of Jesus Christ.

+ We will pursue a rhythm of morning and evening prayers.

+ We will strive to live life with the people on the edges of society—the poor, the forsaken, the oppressed, and the disgraced.

+ As Christ chose for himself a humble life, we will seek to live simply in our affluent culture of over-consumption.

+ We will strive to purify our hearts from the desire for possession and power.

+ Forsaking violence in all of its forms, we will seek and promote peaceful ways of resolving conflict.

We are committed to an incarnational presence on the West Bank.

+ We will spend time understanding the cultures of the West Bank.

+ We will try to get in the way of injustice, especially on the West Bank.

+ We will intentionally build friendships with people on the West Bank.

+ We will remember the people of the West Bank in our daily prayers.

+ We will extend hospitality to our neighbors, sharing what we have with those in need—whether it is a simple meal, clothing, a place to sleep for the night, or our friendship.

We share our lives with one another.

+ We will seek to encounter the living and active person of Jesus Christ in our brothers and sisters.

+ We will regularly attend Missio Dei's gatherings.

+ We will regularly fellowship and pray with members of Missio Dei outside of formal gatherings.

+ We will share resources with those within Missio Dei who demonstrate greater need.

+ We will seek to intercede daily for the other members of Missio Dei.

+ We will pursue reconciliation in our relationships with one another, in our own lives, and in the lives of others in our community.

+ We will discern God's desires for our community communally—seeking God together in prayer, with open hearts.

Missio Dei is a community that is anchored in the Cedar Riverside neighborhood (aka, the West Bank) of Minneapolis. The West Bank is a neighborhood of immigrants, refugees, punks, artists, street folks, students, activists, and professionals (a vast array of humanity in about a square mile). Missio Dei is committed to following Jesus' way of peace, simplicity, prayer, and radical hospitality.

For more information, visit: www.missio-dei.com

This breviary is online at: www.thebreviary.com